The Daily Tel

Hedge Man

The Daily Telegraph

Hedge Man

John Cushnie

Constable • London

Constable & Robinson Ltd
3 The Lanchesters
162 Fulham Palace Road
London W6 9ER
www.constablerobinson.com

First published in the UK by Constable,
an imprint of Constable & Robinson Ltd, 2010

A copy of the British Library Cataloguing in Publication data is available from the British Library

ISBN: 978-1-84901-545-5

Printed and bound in the EU

1 3 5 7 9 10 8 6 4 2

CATG-PEFC-052
www.pefc.org

Contents

Part II
Plants

Part III
Cushnie Design

Part IV
Cushnie Comment

Foreword

I remember clearly the *Gardeners' Question Time* meeting when our then producer, Trevor Taylor, made an announcement as John walked through the door unusually late. John had been stopped for speeding en route but, with his infectious charm, had avoided a charge. The description of the whole encounter caused much hilarity; John was a great raconteur. But that morning John had an even broader grin on his face than usual as Trevor told us all that he was to be a regular writer for the *Daily Telegraph Gardening* supplement.

John loved writing. He wrote exactly as spoke – you can hear his Irish lilt as you read his quips and advice. Many of his observations were accumulated over a long, busy and diverse career in horticulture. What you glean from his pieces is first-hand knowledge laced with generous quantities of his sharp wit and humour. You get a good insight into his likes and dislikes, too: his passion for trees and his loathing of 'rabbit food', as he called greens. But what perhaps comes across most powerfully for me is his generosity of spirit. Whenever you worked with him on any project he would pour his enthusiasm in it. If it was just a germ of a project he would get behind it, help it grow and encourage it, adding his knowledge and expertise to push it on into something capable of taking off. This generosity of spirit is partly why his pieces are so satisfying to read.

Unusually, John did not feel the need to take fashion into account with his approach to gardening. He observed trends come and go and would be quite happy to disagree with a new-fangled idea. He developed his own ideas and techniques based on his in-depth knowledge. His passion for gardening started when his father divided his plot up and gave half to John and half to his brother. John got the bit between his teeth, propagated some plants, sold them and soon had enough to buy his own greenhouse. This led on to studying horticulture at Lurgan College and then Greenmount. He worked for six years with the Northern Ireland Government's horticultural advisory service advising commercial growers on glasshouse crops and fruit.

Working with John was always an enjoyable experience because he was helpful, relaxed and would look out for everyone. He was never self-seeking and was a completely ego-free zone. He could make a large audience hang on his every word whether it was a description of the cultivation of Brussels sprouts or problems with peonies. John is sorely missed on *Gardeners' Question Time*, his Irish brogue and lightning-quick humour combined with his larger-than-life presence are irreplaceable. With this fantastic collection of his writing, though, we can still engage with his warmth, friendliness and honesty – and learn a lot about our plants and gardens to boot.

Bunny Guinness

Introduction

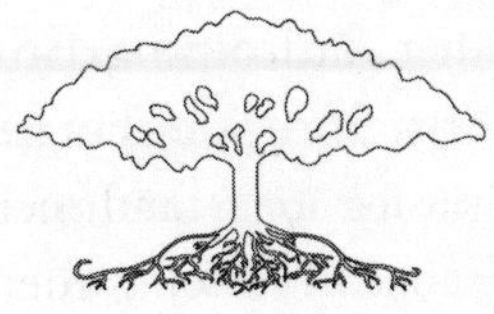

John Cushnie was one of the best, and without question the wittiest, gardening writers in the country. He was also one of the most popular contributors to the *Daily Telegraph Gardening* supplement, and his pieces regularly appeared right from its launch in 2001. His death in December 2009 was a tragedy for all who knew him, and has left a huge gap. This collection of the best of his work over those nine years offers the chance to revisit his pieces, which appear as fresh today as they were when he wrote them.

What made John Cushnie special? If one article sums up his style, it's his advice on sheds (of which he was very fond and had much to say), written in November 2007. It opens, 'There are lots of things that a gardener needs, but the two most important are patience and a shed. Patience will make you a better gardener, but a shed will allow you to make a better garden.' It is witty, pithy and epigrammatical, typical of his style, and perfectly suited to journalism, which – unlike the more meditative pace that books or essays allow – needs a writer who can make a point quickly, efficiently and in a way that entertains the reader.

In fact, John never beat about the bush, and was the master of the one liner. 'A well is for water, a pool is for swimming and – I've always thought – a pond is for plants,' he wrote in May 2003, before describing the best aquatic and marginal plants. He pulls his readers into his articles with vigorous, fast-moving prose that is a joy to read. More than any other gardening writer today, he brought his subject alive – whether the finer points of garden design (he was a landscape designer by profession), the intricacies of planting up a rock garden, or the romance of growing climbers up a tree. He was highly opinionated, often contrary, always off-beat, but dispensed sound horticultural tips and advice with warmth and humour. He was also extremely practical, with a kindly eye for the beginner and expert horticulturist alike.

His writing conveyed great charm. The reader always felt he was on their side. He assumed that they would have modest-sized gardens rather than acres of lawn and vast borders, and that their preoccupations would be with the problems that plague all of us who don't quite have enough space. Included in *Hedge Man* are articles on his solutions to hiding eyesores, making the most of patios, or planting trees for a small garden. His advice, while remaining horticulturally correct, would always offer the simplest most practical route, and he would make even the trickiest job seem easy – 'There is no great secret to making your own living garden maze. Just think of it as a collection of hedges,' he wrote breezily in October 2002. Irresistible. His tip to fellow landscape designers on how to cope with clients always brings a smile to the lips: 'Always give thanks when the "must have" list is sensible and a croquet lawn, hot tub and wild flower meadow have been omitted.'

As well as being a prolific writer, he was familiar to millions as a panellist on Radio 4's *Gardeners' Question Time*. His warm Northern Irish brogue was loved by the millions who listened to him, many of whom would be swept away by his charisma whether they had any interest in gardening or not. His writing perfectly captured his conversational style: 'Far be it from me to complain – especially after last summer's washout,' he opens an article on how to cope with drought in that long rainless spring of 2003, '. . . but please, a little rain would be most welcome. Just a little, no need to overdo it.' You can just hear his playful, cajoling voice. And how well these pieces serve as a diary of the changing seasons and gardening preoccupations.

The title, *Hedge Man*, is apt. When asked by DJ Chris Evans on BBC Radio 2 to comment on his favourite hedges, John Cushnie answered: 'I love yew.' This mischievous response was typical of Cushnie – funny, quick-witted and irreverent – and resulted in Evans nicknaming him 'The Hedge Man'. He was, in fact, very fond of trees and hedges, starting one article with the memorable line, 'I feel sorry for the Leyland cypress. It is certainly ubiquitous and is the cause of much acrimony and worse – but it isn't its fault.'

The book is divided into themes, which quickly emerged when gathering his work together: namely, a section on practical advice, which covers everything from how to make a raised bed to best fertilizers for the garden. The *Daily Telegraph* style remains solidly imperial; when we attempted to turn metric we were inundated with letters from readers who much prefer inches and feet. Cushnie's advice on plants, including trees, shrubs, climbers, herbaceous plants and alpines has a section, as do his articles on design.

Perhaps the most poignant article to appear here is the last he ever wrote, his New Year's resolutions for 2010. It went to press before his death was announced, and appeared days after, on 2 January. It ended: 'One final New Year's Resolution. I am not going to question what I am told. The weather will be as prophesied, the new roses will be resistant to black spot, the tomatoes will have a fantastic flavour and the sweet corn will ripen early. In truth one of the things that make a good gardener is the ability to ignore a lot of nonsense. I hope this wasn't a waste of your time!' It wasn't.

Kylie O'Brien
Gardening Editor
Daily Telegraph

PART I
Practical Cushnie

Talking sheds

There are lots of things that a gardener needs, but the two most important are patience and a shed. Patience will make you a better gardener, but a shed will allow you to make a better garden.

The structure does not have to be new or even attractive – it is simply a weatherproof structure in which to store things. Equally, it is a place to meditate and rest from your labours.

It can double as a potting shed for seed sowing and propagating by cuttings. Now that the weather is growing chilly, a warm shed is a welcome refuge from winter, so give the place a once-over, identify what you really need and, if you are very brave, decide what you should clear out.

What every shed needs

My list may differ from yours but there are some must-haves. Top of the list has to be electricity installed by an electrician. A power point will allow leaf blowers, lawnmowers, hedge trimmers and other power equipment to be operated within cable distance of the shed.

Moreover, light and a heater will make life more enjoyable during cold, dark evenings. But by far the best argument for installing power is the electric kettle. The joy of having a cuppa without having to take off your boots and wash your hands should not be underestimated.

Have a sturdy, waist-high bench or table beside the window. A 6in deep plastic tray with an open front will keep compost where you want it when potting. A great big 6in nail driven into one of the timber corner posts will support wet coats heavy with secateurs, knife, string and other essentials.

It is amazing how many layers of winter clothes gardeners need. None may be fit for a jumble sale but they are familiar and cosy.

Now, call me fussy but there has to be a way of storing boots so they are ready when you need them. I favour the wall rack with deep, narrow V-shapes, each of which supports an upside-down boot. Alternatively, 2ft vertical timber dowel rods spaced 6in apart and attached to a board will do the same job.

An essential piece of furniture is a vermin-proof cupboard or box in which to store seeds. It needs to remain cool but not freezing. If it is strong it may double as a seat.

Tools are the curse of the garden shed. They form a heap, fall over and take up every corner. Invest in a tool rack. There are those gardeners who have every conceivable tool in every style. This causes confusion and you end up spending more time sorting than using. I only use a spade, fork, shovel, two rakes, secateurs, folding hand saw, loppers, a sharpening stone and trowel. I don't have a hoe. In our damp Irish climate, unless you lift and dump the hoed weeds they re-root into the loose soil.

A neat trick is to label each position on the tool rack with the tool that should be in place. That way, if there's a gap, you will know what is missing and can look for it. Otherwise it will eventually turn up rusted and useless.

Make space for sturdy shelves where you can store bulbs. Keep them below eye level to make it easy to check routinely for rotting or diseased bulbs. If the shelves face the window, tubers such as dahlias and begonias may be started into growth in situ.

Leave space on a shelf for essential kit such as labels, string, rooting hormone and soil-testing kit, but keep the area small to prevent clutter.

Clearing out

Now we come to the hard part. If you have had your shed for any length of time it is probably a shambles in need of a serious de-clutter. Start with the obvious. It is time you realized that short bits of string, elastic bands, faded, empty seed packets, bent nails, corks and dried up permanent markers never did have and never will have a use. Broken tools have to go. How many broken, wooden spade shafts can you keep for pointed dibbers when you have used the same perfectly good one for years?

By all means keep some broken clay pots as crocks to aid drainage in other pots. But you have probably hoarded enough to re-pot every plant in the county. They can be stored outside.

Old granular fertilizer should be scattered along the hedge line, or over the compost heap to help it break down. Pesticides that are past their sell-by date should be taken to your local authority for safe, supervised disposal.

Old half-empty bags of potting and seed compost may be scattered over the heather bed. Keep the plastic bags for growing early potatoes on the patio.

Where neatly tied bundles of branches, used as pea supports, are ancient and brittle, leave them out under a hedge or tree for wildlife to move into.

A shed makeover

A shed is a home from home, so by all means personalize it. If the roof is sound then give consideration to a living roof of sedums. They are supplied in carpet form and have proved to be a success at our *Gardeners' Question Time* shed at Sparsholt College, Hampshire.

If it turns you on, by all means have gingham curtains and fancy tie-backs. Personally I have a bolt on the inside of the door, a mug, some gardening magazines, the radio and a cushion (but then I'm a patient gardener).

Stuff to get rid of

Long ago I found that gimmicks put years on you. For instance, I hate bulb-planters. I have never found one that works well on firm, stony ground. Sheep-shear blades always manage to overlap with a gap. And those macho loaded holsters and tool pouches never have the one piece of equipment I need.

How to build your own shed

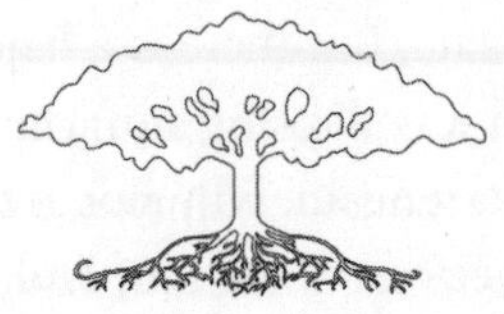

Every garden should have a shed. It's an essential component of a gardener's garden. Often referred to by non-gardeners as a hut, it usually doubles as a potting shed where seeds are sown, perennials divided and the house plants repotted.

The shed provides shelter from the worst of the weather and offers an escape from the pressures of everyday life. It is the store for tools, compost, old catalogues, pots and a collection of completely useless bits and pieces such as broken implements, newspapers, string, brittle pea rods, rusty nails and cracked sheets of glass. All of which must be kept because you never know when they might come in handy.

The garden shed can be cosy as well as practical, with heat, light, an electric kettle and a comfortable seat. More often than not, however, the decorative path leading down to the shed turns to concrete or gravel before reaching the door; and services such as electricity and water also stop short, making it useless at night.

The best kinds used to be the wonderful sheds of the allotments. There was no pretence at achieving a thing of beauty. Cost was the only factor and any material that kept the wind and rain out was put to use.

There is no need for constant tidying. An annual movement of the contents in winter (spring is far too busy a period) is, in my view, more than adequate. But there is a happy balance between a characterful mess and a collapsing tip. There's no need to knock the thing down and start again: why not give it a little attention – smarten the floors, check over the roof and gutters, and generally brighten it up before the autumn damp sets in.

Inside

The floors

If your shed still has a dirt standing and grubby timber duck board, think about laying vinyl, which makes by far the best flooring where lawnmower oil spillage, compost, fertilizer and muddy boots all come together to make a mess. Cut the vinyl 6in larger all round than the floor size. With the corners snipped off, it will curve 3in up each side making brushing out easy with no right angles where the dirt can accumulate.

Walls

Walls are usually made from timber, without the benefit of double skin or insulation. It's well worth attaching polythene or plastic sheeting as an interior skin; the shed will be warmer, less draughty and may even be frost-proof. Inspiring pictures of favourite plants can be used as pin-ups.

Windows

Put wire grills on the outside for security, especially in allotments. Use galvanized mesh, which won't rust.

Ceilings

The inside of a shed roof is not a thing of beauty nor does it need to be. Fix light-weight batons across the roof above head height to support bamboo canes, tree stakes and spare shafts for brushes, rakes and other tools.

Benches

When it is doubling as a potting shed a permanent bench at a suitable height is a must. A 30in-wide tray, 8–9in deep on three sides, open at the front will keep the compost in place. The base should be plastic, vinyl or copper sheet turned over at the edges. Avoid timber, which may cause splinter wounds.

A rack will help keep your tools tidy and available. Install it high enough to hold long-handled rakes and hoes. Well-supported shelves are essential with an area for gardening reference books and plant and seed catalogues as well as pots. A couple of big nails will serve as coat hooks, but space them to prevent the wet, muddy overcoat from contaminating the nice dry jacket.

Where there is an electricity supply each outlet should be fitted with a contact-breaker for safety.

Outside

Paints

There are lots of exterior paints and stains for use on timber in a range of colours. By all means paint the shed blue. It's your shed. But why? I love blue in the garden – blue gentian, ceanothus and poppy all come to mind – but a shed? Trust me; it will stick out like a sore thumb. If you want to avoid green or brown, how about yellow, white or red?

There is no limit to the imagination once you get going. Why not put up imitation or working shutters, or a window box filled with a colourful display of begonias and geraniums? If this is all too twee, try painting a mural.

The door can become a work of art – and you needn't lose the cheerful character of slightly rusted hinges and old-fashioned hook catches. What you should have at the threshold is a sturdy foot scraper – it is both useful and decorative. Place it where you have something to hold as you scrape; it takes effort to dislodge sticky mud from a boot.

Gutters

Where there is a gutter the rainwater can be collected into a wooden barrel. A filter on the end of the downpipe will keep the water free of leaves and debris. A lid will keep mosquitoes at bay. Raise the container on a platform of bricks to a height where a bucket or watering can will fit under the outlet.

The roof

Traditionally the roof is surfaced in tiles or a waterproof membrane such as mineralized felt over timber boards. The small chippings are often green or a dull red-brown. In such cases, climbing plants come into their own. Choose carefully – honeysuckle is pretty and perfumed, and there are several roses, both climbers and ramblers that work well, provided you train the thorns away from the door. The wrong plant will swamp the shed. Avoid the rampant Russian vine *Fallopia baldschuanica*, with its pretty, frothy white summer flowers. Its other common name is mile-a-minute – for good reason. The evergreen *Clematis armandii* and *C. montana* and its varieties are too vigorous for a small shed, as are those famous rose conquerors of open space including 'Kiftsgate', 'Rambling Rector' and 'Wedding Day'.

Living roofs

Mats of flowering sedums appeared on many roofs at Chelsea Flower Show this year. They aren't suitable for a steeply pitched roof, as the surface should be covered with a 2in layer of compost with added polystyrene chips or vermiculite for lightness. This is 'planted' with a mat of sedums, which you can buy rolled up like lawn turf, ready to lay. Water the compost and lay the mat, pegging it in place or covering it with galvanized netting wire.

There are usually five to seven different sedums in the mixture. In flower it can look spectacular – but birds tend to pull pieces out.

More rustic is a sod roof. They are commonplace in Norway and an ideal way of camouflaging a rusting tin roof on the allotment. A layer of grass sods is laid upside down on the roof with another layer of sods grass side up on the top (provided it can take the weight). The grass isn't cut or fertilized. Wild flowers can be encouraged by sowing or transplanting, resulting in a shed with a difference.

How to make a raised bed

Just imagine flavoursome young herbs, succulent, finger-sized carrots and crisp cut-and-come-again lettuce growing without risk from slugs, snails and the dreaded carrot fly. The answer is to grow them in a raised bed. A strip of copper fixed to the top of the surrounding walls will stop the more athletic slugs and snails in their mucus tracks, and banish carrot fly – these low-flyers are afraid of heights, and rarely venture higher than 18–20in. Then there is the advantage of not having to bend down to work. With a bit of planning the bed surround can double as a garden seat.

Position

The site should be in full sun to give the herbs that extra flavour. Existing soil conditions are less important with a raised bed, but avoid a waterlogged area or one contaminated with perennial weeds. If you intend filling it with garden soil, make sure that it hasn't previously been used to grow vegetables. Buy sterilized top-soil to be on the safe side.

Size

Ideally you should be able to reach the centre of the bed from all sides – so 4ft wide is about right for most gardeners. It can be square, rectangular or round (a bit trickier). A comfortable height is about 20in.

Materials

The walls can be made from timber such as scaffolding planks, available from salvage yards. Drive 4in long square posts into the ground at the corners and space them every 3ft along the sides. Two planks placed above each other and fixed with screws to the outside of the posts should be the right height. Don't be tempted to use old railway sleepers – the very old ones may exude creosote, which you don't want anywhere near where food is being grown.

A concrete block or brick structure bonded with mortar can be built – or have a go with interlocking, coloured concrete bricks. They are as easy to build as Lego, locking together to form a solid 9in wide wall without any need for mortar.

Dig a 6in deep trench, 12in wide, and back-fill it with consolidated broken stone. Surface with fine stone. Lay the interlocking bricks using a spirit level to make sure the bottom row is level. The top of a solid wall can be finished with either a pre-formed coping stone or flat patio tiles set in mortar. Let the coping overhang the outside of the wall by 2in. This will be wide enough to use as a seat.

Soil

When filling the raised bed, try to include a layer of old, well-rotted farmyard manure in the base to retain moisture. Add coarse, washed grit to help drainage and to allow the soil to warm up more quickly. Mix bone meal at 2oz per sq yd into the top layer and allow the soil to settle. After a few days top up with a 2in layer of potting compost.

Don't waste valuable space on bulky herbs. Rosemary and sage can be planted in a mixed shrub or herbaceous border. Alternatively, plant a young specimen and keep it clipped. Thyme can be left to grow over the coping or timber, softening the edge – but it will also act as a drawbridge over the copper strip for slugs and snails.

Early carrots and spring onions will love the soil conditions and a few onion sets for autumn harvesting will grow between the herbs and lettuce. Basil can be started indoors in pots and plunged into the raised bed after June.

Remember to order the building blocks, coping tiles and soil for delivery before Saturday morning. By late afternoon you can pay a visit to the plant centre for the herbs and seeds.

How to build a rain reservoir

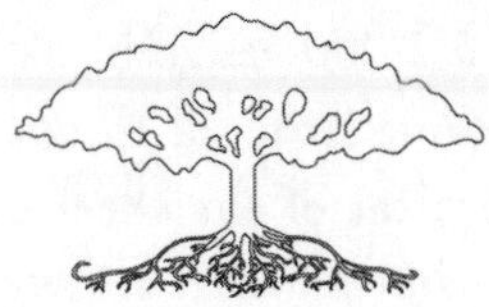

When collecting water, size matters. The larger the area, the more you catch. Select a level site on solid ground. Choose a position close to where the water will be needed, and preferably in the open to catch as much rain as possible.

Construction

Build the reservoir above ground so you can draw off the water. The sides need to be strong to withstand the sideways pressure of the stored water. It doesn't have to be a permanent fixture. Use railway sleepers laid flat on solid, level ground. Select straight sleepers and lay one on top of the other, interlocking at the corners to add stability and strength. Make the walls secure by driving timber stakes into the ground, tight against the outsides. Use two 4in round stakes per sleeper length. Sleepers vary in thickness, but building them four-high on each side will make a reservoir approximately 11 sq ft and 3ft high, holding 1,875 gallons – that's nearly 1,000 buckets – of water.

Waterproofing

Cover the ground within the walls with a layer of sand to prevent the liner being punctured by the weight of the water pressing on sharp stones. Use a 1,000-gauge black polythene sheet with an underskirt of the same material to cover the rough sides of the sleepers. Fold the pleat of the sheet inwards at the corners to make a neat tuck, and allow it to overhang the top of the walls.

Cut a length of flexible hose long enough to reach the base of the liner and overhang the outside to ground level. The larger the diameter of hose, the faster the flow of water. Fit a tap to the free end and secure the other end 1in clear of the bottom of the reservoir. Set the end on a tile and hold it firmly in place by tying it to a couple of bricks. Raising the inlet a little above the base will stop debris blocking the flow.

Once a few inches of water have been collected in the reservoir, hold the tap end of the hose above the water level and plug the other end. With the tap open, pour water into the hose until it is full. Turn off the tap and lower the end. When you unplug the end in the water and open the tap, water should flow out of the reservoir, using a siphoning action.

If you can exclude daylight there will be less risk of algae. Black landscape fabric is porous, allowing water to percolate through. Stretch a layer across the top and hold it in place with battens that can be screwed to the top line of the sleepers. Alternatively, form a tent of black polythene sheeting draped over a horizontal pole supported on timber uprights. The two sides of the sheeting can be fixed to timber roofing laths and nailed to the sleepers, leaving a 3in gap for the water to run off into the reservoir.

Safety

Consider very carefully the safety aspect. You should either fence the area or fit wire mesh to cover the whole reservoir, supported by steel rods or poles.

If you haven't the time, or don't fancy carrying buckets of water across the garden, connect up some leaky hose to run to the most needy areas. The tap can be connected to each line of hose in turn.

Extra tips

- If your butts are low on water, increase their catchment area by adding a collar to the top rim of the butt, which will act rather like a large funnel. Sheets of hardboard or plywood covered in polythene and angled towards the top of the butt or barrel will direct the water.
- The soil at the base of a wall is always dry. A 12in-wide strip can be completely missed by the rain, and because the foundations are often rubbly, these factors can cause wall plants and climbers to suffer.
- Where there is a downpipe from the guttering close to the corner of the gable, rainwater can be re-directed along the base of the wall. However, do ensure that the damp-proof course is above soil level.
- Use a length of half-round guttering, drilling 5mm holes along its length. Fit end pieces at either end and place it along the

wall, raised off the ground on two or three bricks. Direct the bottom of the downpipe into the gutter so that when it rains, it will keep the soil moist.

Choosing the right fertilizer for your plants

This season, trees, shrubs and even lawns have grown phenomenally well. Much of the young growth is lush and soft and will be prone to frost – so, to harden up the shoots before the frost, feed them now with a high potash liquid fertilizer.

But take care: overfed plants haven't the luxury of exercise. They may grow faster, produce more leaves, flower better, yield lots of fruit or go to seed, yet applying the wrong combination of nutrients to a plant can be a disaster.

The three main nutrients in most fertilizer mixtures are nitrogen (N), phosphate (P205) and potash (K). Some plant food mixtures, such as rose fertilizer, will contain small amounts of minor (trace) elements, especially magnesium and iron. When these are in short supply or not available it may lead to a yellow mottling or discolouring of the leaves.

Nitrogen will encourage a plant to make growth. It is useful for the lawn and for leafy vegetables such as cabbage; however, too much of it will produce leaves and growth at the expense of flowers and fruit.

Phosphate will ensure the plant's growth is sturdy and will assist in the formation of a good root system. Root vegetables, especially carrots, benefit from an application of a high phosphate fertilizer.

Potash fertilizer helps the plant to produce healthy flowers and fruit.

A balanced fertilizer will contain all three nutrients, with adjustments in quantities for the different needs of specific plants.

Brassicas enjoy a lime-rich soil (a pH above 7). It is usually applied as calcium (Ca) in the autumn on ground that has been dug over. Lime also works wonders breaking up heavy clay soils.

While lime is tolerated by some plants such as *Ceanothus*, lilac and box hedging, lime-hating, ericaceous plants need an alkaline-free, acid soil. These include rhododendron, camellia and *Pieris*.

There is often confusion over the role played by organic matter or humus in the garden. You don't have to be an organic grower to appreciate the benefits of well-rotted farmyard manure and good home-made compost or leaf mould. They are superb soil conditioners, which help to retain moisture while opening up heavy clay soils. They are, however, low in nutrients. A handful of artificial, general-purpose fertilizer will contain more nitrogen, phosphate and potash than a wheelbarrow of farmyard manure. If you are not growing organically then a combination of organic material and artificial fertilizer will keep most plants happy.

Bone meal (phosphate), seaweed fertilizer (nitrogen and trace elements), blood, fish and bone meal (balanced), wood ash (potash) and ground rock potash (potash) are organic fertilizers.

How they are sold

Garden centres supply both organic and inorganic fertilizers. Some are easier to apply and more quickly available than others. Powdered fertilizers such as bone meal are apt to adhere to wet leaves. They are best applied to and cultivated into the topsoil before planting. Fertilizers sold in granular form are useful for scattering through plants. It bounces off the foliage, dissolving on the ground after rain. A soluble fertilizer will readily dissolve in water and is immediately available to the plant through its roots.

Fertilizers in liquid form are diluted and applied either to the soil to be taken up through the roots, or as a foliar feed absorbed through the plant's leaves.

Slow-release fertilizers are ideal for shrubs and trees. They discharge their nutrients over a stated period of up to 12 months.

Single-nutrient fertilizers are used to increase the level of one element for a particular need of the plant – sulphate of potash, for instance, is applied in winter to the base of fruit trees to encourage extra flowers and fruit.

Liquid organic fertilizers may be made from animal manure or comfrey leaves allowed to rot in water for four to six weeks. The resultant liquid is diluted and used instead of artificial fertilizer – but it is difficult to know exactly what type and quantity of nutrients are being applied.

Golden rules for using fertilizers

- Store fertilizers safely.
- Always follow the manufacturer's instructions.
- Giving more fertilizer than the recommended dose will do the plant more harm than good. Where too much has been

given, drench the soil or compost with water to flush out the excess.

- Feed tender, outdoor plants with a high-potash feed in early autumn to harden up the young growths before frost causes damage.
- When applying a granular fertilizer to dry soil, water it in well.
- Never apply fertilizer in winter when plants are dormant or when they are in waterlogged soil conditions.
- To avoid over-feeding make a note of when you fertilized the lawn.

Winter containers and hanging baskets

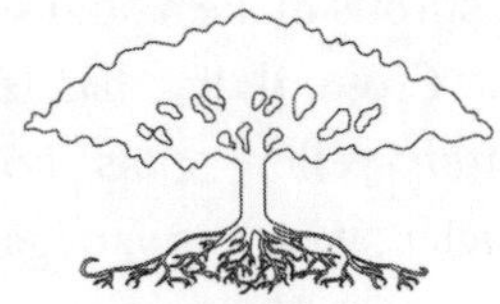

There's nothing more cheery over Christmas than a beautifully arranged hanging basket or a tub, full of hardy plants that look good even in the bleakest mid-winter. They are surprisingly easy to keep and you can transfer many of the plants to the garden when they outgrow their container.

Plants

Thyme, mint, sage, lavender and even parsley can all play a part in hanging baskets and containers. *Buxus sempervirens*, which is more usually seen as dwarf hedging, makes an excellent centrepiece in an arrangement of low-growing winter-flowering polyanthus. One-year-old, well-rooted cuttings of forsythia will provide a bold splash of bright yellow and Hebes such as *H. ochracea* 'James

Stirling', which has old-gold stems, and *H.* × *franciscana* 'Variegata', with its dark evergreen leaves edged with white, also make a bold display. *Eleagnus fortunei* 'Emerald and Green' has small green-and-cream evergreen and pink-tinged foliage in winter, and can be planted out in the garden after a few seasons when it has got too big for the pot.

Dwarf and slow-growing conifers, including *Juniperus communis* 'Compressa', (dwarf) and *Chamaecyparis* 'Elwoodii', are great for creating height in an arrangement of winter-flowering pansies, and young, leafy evergreen shrubs make a bold statement. The spotted laurel, *Aucuba japonica* 'Crotonifolia', has large, glossy evergreen leaves dotted with buttery-yellow spots. Ivies are useful: a good one is *Hedera helix* 'Glacier', which is variegated with small leaves. The periwinkles *Vinca minor* 'Variegata' and *V. major* 'Variegata', together with *Ajuga reptans* 'Multicolor', better known as the bugle plant, keep their foliage throughout winter.

Bulk out the basket with coloured fillers such as polyanthus and pansies and winter-flowering heathers such as the white *Erica* × *darleyensis* 'Silberschmelze', and *E. carnea* 'Springwood Pink'. Dwarf, early-flowering corms such as hardy cyclamen will also brighten up a container: try *C. hederifolium* and *C. coum*.

Soil

Buy a ready-made compost. Soil-based mixtures are heavier and more moisture-retentive; this is an advantage where pots are in a windy position and liable to be blown over. Peat or peat-free soil-less composts are less prone to freezing in the container. There is no need for fertilizer; the compost should contain enough nutrients to see plants through the winter. A single application of a balanced liquid fertilizer in early spring will keep them going.

All containers should have at least one drainage hole in the base. Cover the hole, inside, with pieces of broken clay pots or polystyrene to prevent it blocking or the compost washing out. Water after planting to settle the compost round the roots; only add water if it loses moisture after that.

Position

Place baskets out of harm's way, sheltered from the worst of the wind and rain. Avoid areas of deep shade or where the cold air is tunnelled between high walls creating turbulence and causing baskets to swing wildly.

Coloured ribbons and tinsel add colour to dull earthenware pots. Sprigs of berried and variegated holly pushed into the compost add green and provide visiting birds with food.

How to cope with drought

Far be it from me to complain – especially after last summer's washout – but please, a little rain would be most welcome. Just a little, no need to overdo it.

Some gardeners on the eastern side of the country haven't experienced serious rain for a month. A light drizzle, equivalent to a heavy dew, didn't do any good as it evaporated off the soil surface next morning. The ground has become bone dry and, where it is heavy loam or clay, surface cracks are causing problems when sowing seeds.

Vulnerable plants

New plantings made over the winter months are particularly vulnerable to long periods of drought. Until their roots spread out into undisturbed soil they have to rely on water at hand. Once that is exhausted the new growth of plants slows right down and root action ceases so they eventually wilt and die.

In some areas even established herbaceous perennials are slow to break into growth. Fruit trees rely on spring rain to top up the ground water they need once growth commences. Any shortage during the time when the small fruitlets are starting to swell may cause them to abort, resulting in little or no crop. Raspberries are surface-rooting and are unable to go deep in search of water. Next years' fruiting canes should be growing strongly now – without reasonable soil moisture they will be stunted, giving less fruit next summer.

It's not all doom and gloom, however. Some plants are in their element: lavender loves it hot and dry, repaying us with increased fragrance; *Cytisus* (broom) and *Genista*, such as the lovely yellow-flowering *G. lydia* and *G. hispanica*, succeed best in a dry, free-draining soil.

Better still, the weeds are less aggressive and those that are removed with a hoe are less likely to re-root into hard dry soil.

Take action

Beds mulched during the winter will be better able to withstand long periods without rain. The surface coating of bark, compost or gravel will conserve moisture with less evaporation. The problem is with recently planted beds that are ready for a mulch. There is little point in applying it to dry soil. If it does rain the bark will prevent the water reaching the soil, making the problem worse.

If you do water, apply sufficient to do some good: 10 minutes with a sprinkler is worse than useless. Allow the water to wet the top 6in, turning the soil with a spade to check how deep it has penetrated. A mulch can be applied once the soil is wet.

Planting tips

Easter Monday is one of the busiest days in the garden-centre calendar. If the weather is warm and sunny sales will rocket and gardens will be the better for it providing you keep to a few simple, common-sense rules.

- When you bring the plants home check that the compost is moist. If it is dry plunge the plant, pot and all, into water until it ceases to produce bubbles. Allow the surplus water to drain off. If you can't plant immediately then stand the pot in a sheltered, shady spot where you won't forget to water it.
- Prepare the planting pit the previous day, making it larger than the pot. Fill the hole with water and allow it to drain down into the ground.
- Mix moisture-retentive compost into the topsoil to be spread around the roots.
- Firm the soil down well, keeping the plant at the same soil level as it was in the container.
- Dish the surface of the soil towards the stem of the plant to direct rainwater where it will be of most use.
- Continue to water the plant as often as necessary and damp the foliage in the morning to reduce water loss.

How to prune

Most plants benefit from a short back and sides. The results can be spectacular: pruning helps maintain a pleasing compact shape while encouraging flowers, stem colour and leaf growth.

Usually when you cut a young branch the plant responds by sending out two or three side shoots. Shrubs such as *Escallonia, Philadelphus* and *Olearia* will produce new growths from old branches that have been cut down to stumps. But beware: pruning hard back into old wood is not always successful. Some conifers simply won't recover.

Trees

Trees and shrubs with brightly coloured bark can be encouraged to produce more of the same. With *Cornus* (dogwood) and *Salix* (willow) it is the new growth produced during the year that has the brightest winter and spring bark. Dogwoods such as *Cornus alba*

'Sibirica', with bright-red bark, and *C. sanguinea* 'Winter Beauty', resplendent in stems of orange-yellow with red at the tips, are best pruned annually in spring. Cut the stems to 6in from the ground.

The willow, *Salix alba* subsp. *vitellina* 'Chermesina', produces carmine-red winter stems. It can be coppiced close to the ground every other spring. When pruned higher up the trunk it builds up a head of coloured branches.

Betula utilis var. *jacquemontii* is often planted in isolation to draw the eye to its brilliant-white bark. When planted in a group of other trees it seems to light up its neighbours.

The foxglove tree *Paulownia tomentosa* is quick-growing, forming a large 40ft-high tree with hairy bright-green leaves up to 12in long. It can be grown in confined areas by pruning annually in spring to within 12in of the ground. Vigorous, stoutly vertical 10ft-high stems will be produced with exceptionally large 18in leaves. There won't be a show of the fragrant pink-lilac flowers – these only appear on trees at least 10 years old – but the display of foliage will more than compensate.

The Indian bean tree, *Catalpa bignonioides*, and the golden-leafed variety *C. b.* 'Aurea' can be coppiced in early spring in the same way as the *Paulownia*. This will produce large leaves for summer.

When coppiced, *Eucalyptus gunnii* produces silvery-blue, juvenile 'penny' foliage where the stem appears to be in the centre of rounded leaves. After a few seasons of coppicing the new shoots need to be thinned in spring to prevent the plant becoming an overcrowded thicket.

Flowering shrubs

The pruning method used to achieve maximum flowering will depend on the growth habit of any particular shrub.

In summer the magnificent *Hydrangea paniculata* produces large conical panicles of creamy-white flowers on the new growth made that season. Prune in early spring, removing all the previous years' stems to within a few buds of the older branches. The new shoots should produce large terminal panicles within 8 to 10 weeks.

Forsythia has a different method of flowering, producing its golden display in late winter and early spring on stems from the previous year. After flowering prune the branches back to young growths lower down the stem or immediately above strong growth buds. The shoots produced will grow during the season and flower the following spring.

The winter- and early spring-flowering heathers such as *Erica carnea* and *E.* × *darleyensis* are pruned as soon as the flowers have faded. Clip them over with hedge clippers or secateurs, removing the dead heads. The new shoots – which will produce next year's flowers – will appear in late spring.

If the old flowers are allowed to remain, new growths will form beyond them making the plant appear straggly.

Clematis

The pruning regime for clematis depends on the species and the time of flowering for hybrid varieties.

Those needing little or no pruning include the evergreen *Clematis armandii* and *C. cirrhosa* together with the well-known and vigorous *C. montana* and *C. macropetala*. If they outgrow their allotted space or become untidy they may be hard-pruned immediately after they have finished flowering.

Then there are the lovely early, large flowering varieties which produce their flowers in May and early June. They flower on short shoots from the previous year's growth. Simply cut back dead and weak stems to just above a healthy bud in early spring.

The large-flowering hybrids and varieties of *C. viticella* and *C. orientalis* that flower in June should have already been hard-pruned (February or early March is best). Working up each stem from the base, remove all the growth above the first pair of healthy fat buds.

Pruning tips

- Make sure all cutting equipment is sharp.
- Don't prune during frosty weather.
- Cut immediately above a bud or side shoot to prevent dieback.
- Whenever possible make a sloping cut away from the bud to allow the water to run off.
- The way the bud is pointing is the direction the resultant shoot will grow.
- Prune as low as possible if you want to encourage new growth from the base.
- Feed after pruning to encourage growth.

How to hide unsightly garden features

Almost all gardens have some kind of hideous object or structure that is a blot on the landscape, and which simply begs to be disguised. Making the monstrosity disappear from view, while adding overall interest and colour to the garden, is a simple Saturday job.

Planting

Achieve instant disguise by planting an evergreen shrub directly in front of the eyesore, or screening it off with container-grown columnar conifers. Select reasonably sized, slow-growing species, such as the Irish yew, *Taxus baccata* 'Fastigiata', or the Irish juniper, *Juniperus communis* 'Hibernica'. Keep the compost 2in below the container's rim to allow watering and liquid feeding.

Planting pot-grown specimen bamboos can also provide instant screening. Or surround the object with curved beds that draw the eye away from the centre. Bulky, quick-growing shrubs such as the aromatic evergreen *Choisya ternata* and fragrant-flowering *Mahonia* × *media* 'Winter Sun' will soon block the view.

Attention to detail at the time of planting will speed up the growth of the camouflaging plants. The roots of container-grown plants should be teased out from the ball of compost. Dig the planting hole larger than the root ball and fork up the bottom to loosen the subsoil and make root penetration easier. Separate the clay subsoil from the topsoil and discard the subsoil. A layer of compost or rotted manure in the base of the hole will help to retain moisture close to the roots. Mix a handful of granular fertilizer through the topsoil before pushing it firmly around the roots.

Fencing

Unless care is taken with the design, a screening fence will be seen for what it is – a wooden fence around an eyesore. In some instances, this might even be worse than looking at the object you are attempting to disguise.

To build an attractive screen, use 4in square supporting posts for 5–6ft high overlap fencing panels. Dig holes about 2ft deep × 1ft wide. Use concrete to set the posts in position, leaving them a minimum of 8ft above ground.

Attach lengths of hemp rope 2in in diameter to the top of the remaining posts, looped between each like swags. Rambler or climbing roses planted at the base of the fence can then be trained to cover the panels and up and along the rope. No one will stop to think what is on the other side of the fence. The box-like shape may be altered by an extra panel set at an angle. You could even hide a compost heap behind it.

Materials

All the plants can be ordered from your local garden centre or nursery. For the timber screen, the posts should be 4in square and 10ft long.

The posts and panels should be purchased pre-treated with preservative. You will need half a cubic metre of concrete for every 10 posts. Leave a gap of 2in between the concrete and ground level. When the concrete is set firm it can be covered with soil. Don't nail on the panels for a few days until the concrete has hardened. Use non-rusting galvanized nails, and a spirit level to ensure the posts are straight.

You can get the hemp rope from a good hardware store or a ship's chandler.

How to conceal compost heaps and oil tanks

Not all is sitting pretty in the garden. Equipment for composting lurks in dark corners, and oil or gas tanks sit in clear view. In some cases, the boiler itself lives in the garden. As a consequence, camouflaging the less presentable accoutrements of house and home is an important aspect of garden design. It is not wise to 'stick' everything under a tree in the far corner of the garden. (That area is better kept as a quiet, sheltered spot, or for growing shade-loving plants.)

Oil and gas tanks need to be readily accessible and in easy reach of the delivery lorry (some truck drivers seem to be programmed to trail pipes over plants).

Storage for other fuels, such as firewood and coal, can be provided by a coal bunker. There are some fairly attractive designs available, but they still tend to stand out wherever they are positioned.

Refuse bins are not pleasing to the eye, either. Unfortunately they need to be close to the kitchen door – though far enough away to keep unpleasant odours at bay.

Composting on a grand scale is common in gardens, with bins, tumblers and purpose-built compost heaps taking up considerable space. The composting site needs to be central, to ease the collection of debris and the eventual return of the lovely, crumbly, peat-like compost to the borders and beds. A path leading to the site is essential for transporting the raw ingredients.

Objects that are not only unsightly and difficult to camouflage but also fixed in place are the bane of many a garden. With a new house, the siting of manhole covers, electricity and telephone poles – and, in rural gardens, the septic tank – needs to be discussed with the architect at an early stage. If manhole covers can be placed in shrub beds, they will be accessible but hidden from view.

Concealed sites

A blind spot in the garden can be a great asset. Many houses have an area behind the garage that is hidden from all the windows. Make this your glory hole, your landfill site. Screen it from the garden and make it a no-go area for all but your nearest and dearest.

If you don't make compost and don't have oil or gas tanks, this area can be reserved for the nuts and bolts of gardening: bales of peat, bags of grit and compost, wire netting, bamboo canes and all the other essentials that are banned from the garage.

Camouflage

If you spread unsightly objects about the garden and screen them properly, most will escape the notice of non-gardeners (though a good gardener will still spot the oil tank under the clematis).

Plants give the most natural-looking camouflage, but also useful are timber fences, lattice screens and walls of brick or stone. Screens made of these materials will benefit from a covering layer of plants.

A living screen

A hedge is the ideal way to hide anything in the garden. Formal hedges, such as privet and yew, need regular clipping to keep them tidy and under control, but informal shrub hedges require only a little pruning and tend to form broader hedges.

You'll need a gap wide enough for a wheelbarrow, ideally positioned at one end of the hedge so that anyone looking through the gap sees only more hedge. Alternatively, plant one side of the hedge about 4ft in front of the other side so that it overlaps and conceals the gap.

Evergreen shrubs that don't require regular pruning make an effective permanent screen. It is amazing what can be hidden behind a mature, large, hybrid rhododendron or a bushy camellia.

Making timber screens

Panel fences, trellis fences and vertical-board fences can be used to screen refuse bins and storage areas.

To make a panel fence, use 4in×4in treated timber fence posts and either mount them in proprietary metal fence spikes driven into the ground, or dig post holes and concrete the posts in, checking with a spirit level that they are plumb. Secure the fence panels to the posts using galvanized nails.

For vertical-board fencing, the boards – each 5–6ft high, 6in wide and 1in thick – are nailed top and bottom to two parallel,

3in×2in runners fixed between the upright posts. The boards are spaced 1in apart to allow air through.

Timber screens can be stained to help them blend in with their surroundings. Use them as support for climbers and plant free-standing shrubs in front.

Training plants over tanks

Use galvanized netting wire to cover plastic or metal fuel tanks. Staple 1in×1in timber batons to the netting, roughly 2ft apart, and then drape the wire mesh over the tank with the batons between the wire and the tank; this leaves space for climbing plants to scramble through the wire.

Place timber pegs in the ground and secure the netting to the pegs. Before driving the pegs in firmly, be sure to mark the position of the outlet fuel pipe.

Manholes and septic tanks

It is likely that at some stage they will become blocked and it will be necessary to open manholes. If they are hidden too well you may forget their location and end up digging most of the garden to find them. In patio areas, fit a recessed manhole lid flush with the surrounding surface, and simply put a large wooden barrel or a planted container on top to disguise it. For instant access, simply move the container.

Gravelling the surface of the septic tank or manhole is an effective camouflage, and the gravel is easily removed for access. When you need to find the manhole cover again, just stamp your foot on the gravel and listen for a hollow sound.

Making a compost container

Aeration is essential when making compost, so the container needs to have holes in the sides and in the base to ensure adequate movement of air. A strong, well-built container will last for years.

An area 6ft×6ft is about the right size, and the container should be roughly 5ft high.

Make a wooden container by driving four 4in square corner posts into the ground (use pressure-treated timber that will not rot). To make up three sides of the container, fix 6in×1in planks with a 1in gap between them for air to flow. The fourth side should be removable, for access to the compost.

To make slots in which the removable side will run, use galvanized nails to attach a pair of 1in×1in battens down the inside faces of the posts, leaving a 2in gap between the battens. Then simply slide 6in×1in boards down the grooves made by the battens.

Raising the base on bricks lets air penetrate under the heap. The waterproof lid may be made from carpet nailed on a wooden frame and covered with polythene. Corrugated plastic sheets are light for lifting when filling.

The simplest sort of compost container consists of four round timber corner posts, each 6½ft long, 3in in diameter, and pointed at one end. Drive the posts 18in into the ground, leaving 5ft of post above ground. Staple on 1in mesh wire netting to make the four sides. The mesh will let air enter the heap and keep the compost from spilling out.

Design tips for successful compost

- Build the materials in layers no more than 9in deep.
- Don't try to compost the roots of perennial weeds.

- Add a nitrogen-rich activator such as poultry manure.
- Turn the compost regularly.
- Never let the material dry out.

How to fake a stone trough for alpine plants

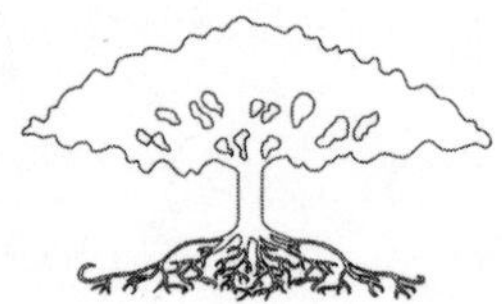

An old-fashioned drinking trough cut from solid stone makes an ideal container for displaying alpines, but they can be very expensive. The answer is to fake it – by making concrete look naturally weather-worn and very old. The easiest to copy is a porous rock known as tufa.

As with any container, the ideal size will be determined by its weight. Don't be too ambitious: a trough 20in long, 18in wide and 6in deep will be quite heavy to move.

Materials

- You will need: 25kg (55lb) cement, 25kg (55lb) coarse sand, 100 litres of sphagnum moss
- Thin plywood sheet 20in×18in×1in

- Galvanized wire mesh 24in×16in
- Two 2in long pieces of 1in diameter dowel rod (or sections of broom handle)

Method

Choose an area of the garden where the surface is flat and the soil is firm loam or clay, and free from large stones. Mark out the size of the trough using string, ensuring the corners form right angles. Dig a hole 20in×18in×6in, keeping the sides perpendicular. Level the base and lay the plywood sheet down. Coat the upper side with grease to prevent the mixture sticking to the wood. Next, make an open-topped wooden box 16in×14in ×4in.

Alternatively, you could buy a metal or plastic box of similar dimensions. Thoroughly mix the dry cement and sand. Add it to the sphagnum moss and mix well to form hyper-tufa. Dampen the mixture but don't let it become too wet.

Spread the hyper-tufa 1in deep over the plywood base. Take the wire mesh and bend the two short sides at right angles 2in from the end. Place it on the base with the ends pointing up. This will help to reinforce the base and the lower sides of the trough. Add another 1in layer of the mixture.

Grease and push in the wooden dowels 12in apart to form drainage holes. Grease the outside surfaces of the box and position it in the hole with equal clearance on all sides. The finished trough will have sides 2in thick.

Back-fill with the hyper-tufa mixture, pushing it into the gap between the soil and the box. Use a piece of wood as a rammer, making sure there are no air pockets and the mixture is in contact with the sides of the hole. Level all around the top of the 'walls' with a spirit level. Cover it to protect it from rain and leave until next weekend.

Take out the inner box and excavate the surrounding soil to remove the trough. Lift out the plywood sheet to leave a smooth, level base. Push out the two dowel rods and make the two holes neat and clean for drainage. The outside of the trough will be roughened, having taken the shape of the side walls of the hole in the ground.

Once you've got the trough out, hose it down and use a stiff brush to remove any soil or stones. It should look old and well worn. Allow the trough to 'cure' for another week by raising it off the ground on bricks or blocks.

Planting

Cover the drainage holes on the inside with pieces of broken slate to prevent the compost falling through. Use an open, gritty, free-draining, soil-based compost.

You can now plant the trough with miniature conifers such as *Juniperus communis* 'Compressa' or a selection of choice alpines. Try gentians, *Daphne oleoides* or *Lewisia cotyledon* hybrids. The soil surface can be dressed with pieces of tufa or fine gravel.

Don't forget to fill the hole in the ground, unless you fancy having a matching pair of almost-antique stone troughs.

How to prevent waterlogging

Waterlogging is common with clay soils because the fine particles stick together and prevent water from moving. One answer is to dig over the soil with organic materials such as compost, leaf mould and peat – or to incorporate grit and fine gravel – which will open the texture.

Waterlogging also occurs where the topsoil forms a shallow layer overlying rock or chalk. Raising the level of the soil may help the water to drain more quickly.

Beware, also, in areas where the ground has become compacted – on a lawn that is heavily used, for instance. Rainwater will tend to lie on the surface rather than percolate to a lower level. Spiking the lawn, using a hollow-tine aerator (available to hire and easy to use), will puncture the crust, removing small plugs of soil. Brush coarse grit over the surface to fill these vertical channels – thus keeping them open.

Forking ground for planting will open the soil and may eliminate the problem altogether. When using a spade or digging fork work backwards, turning the soil you have been standing on. Leave large clods to be broken down by winter frost and wind.

Laying pipes

If, however, the ground remains in a marshy condition for long periods the solution may be to drain the area. Get to know your garden layout. Check if there is an outlet where the water can escape – a nearby ditch or stream would be ideal. Take care not to deflect the water and flood a neighbouring property.

Digging drains is hard, slow work that causes disruption until complete. The quantity and the pattern of the drains will depend on the size of the area and the type of soil. With heavy, clay soils they will need to be closer together – a herring-bone pattern will probably be ideal, with one main drain running the full length of the problem area. Side drains (laterals) should run into it, in the direction of the flow, at a 45 degree angle. Where the laterals are on both sides of the drain they should be staggered so that they don't enter from opposite sides at the same place.

Where the drains are cutting through a lawn, remove the turf and store outside, the right way up, in a sheltered position. Excavate a straight trench, starting at the outlet and working back through the area to be drained. The outlet should be the lowest point, with the base of the trench rising towards the far end.

The recommended fall (slope) is 1:40. This means a 40ft length of drain will be 12in lower at the outlet. The trench should be at least 10in deep at the start of the fall.

As you dig, separate the topsoil from the subsoil. When the trench is clean lay a 3in or 4in diameter slit-plastic drainage pipe in the base. Place larger stones over the length of the pipe to stop it from rising out of the trench before it can be covered.

Back-fill over the pipe with a 3–4in layer of clean, broken stones that are 1–2in in size. Replace the topsoil, leaving it slightly higher to allow for settlement. Where the grass turf was lifted, firm the soil and replace the stored turf leaving it slightly higher. Dump any subsoil, taking care not to destroy the lawn when wheeling it away. Surface water should now percolate the soil and the stones will trap any debris likely to clog the slits in the pipe. If the fall is correct, water should exit the end of the pipe and drain out of your life for ever.

Build a sump

Where there is no outlet and the waterlogged area is small, the answer may be to construct a sump – which, again, involves a fair bit of back-breaking digging.

Excavate a hole as large as 6ft square and 3–4ft deep. Dump the subsoil. Fill the hole with large stones to within 9in of the surface. Leave lots of gaps between this hardfill and cover it with landscape fabric to prevent soil washing back into these holes.

Back-fill with the topsoil, leaving the finished level a few inches above the surface to allow for settlement of the soil. Rainwater from the surrounding area will drain into the sump, from which it can seep away over time.

An alternative is to import and spread topsoil to raise the finished level above the water table. Raised beds will allow crops to be grown successfully with their roots above the wet ground.

Water-loving plants

If all else fails, the answer may be to plant the area with varieties that enjoy wet conditions. Large trees such as willow, alder, rowan, snowy mespilus and birch will tolerate wet soil and help to dry out the ground. They absorb the water through their roots and expel it through their foliage into the air.

The red-and-yellow-stemmed dogwoods (*Cornus*) will grow with their feet in water, as will the edible cranberry and cowberry (*vaccinium*).

Where space allows plant a dawn redwood, *Metasequoia glyptostroboides*. It thrives in wet ground, quickly growing to 30–40ft, and has deciduous foliage that turns butter-yellow in autumn.

Submerged plants

Where gardens suffer from serious flooding plants may have to contend with deep water. Here the choice is limited. In winter, when they are without leaves, *Hydrangea macrophylla*, *Chaenomeles japonica*, *Viburnum farreri*, *Cornus alba* and *Sambucus nigra* will all survive being submerged for up to a week. After the flood water recedes wash mud and silt off the stems. Later, in early summer, apply a balanced fertilizer to replace nutrients washed out of the ground.

How to build a pond

The fascination with water is something few of us grow out of. The shimmering surface of a garden pond throws back teasing reflections of the plants, birds and insects that make it their home, which is why it is such an important ingredient in an exciting, vibrant garden.

Ponds must complement their surroundings. A good rule of thumb for formal areas, such as a lawn or paved area, is to construct a similarly formal pond: a sunken circle, square or rectangle. Where the style is informal, the only limit to the size and shape is the amount of space available.

Gentle curves make interesting shapes but remember that you also want to be able to enjoy the pond from inside the house as well as from the terrace. So mark out the shape with sand or the garden hose and check it out from every angle, including from an upstairs window, before excavating.

Standing water is naturally found at the lowest part of a landscape and that is where it looks best. But unnatural garden ponds often break this law. Do choose a level site, though, to avoid the need for retaining walls.

Areas where the water table rises after heavy rain are bad news as the hole may fill up, displacing the liner and the bulk of the water. As the water table recedes, the liner falls back into place, leaving the pool nearly empty. Lastly, large trees bring problems, too. Cut roots may regrow and puncture the liner. Falling leaves are another nuisance. And dense shade will restrict plant growth.

Pond lining

Spread a 2in layer of fine sand over the base and sides to cushion the liner from sharp stones. With rocky ground, you may need to use a layer of purpose-made underlay or a piece of old carpet.

Spread the liner over the hole, taking care not to let any stones fall in on top of the sand, and use bricks around the edge to hold the liner in place.

As you start to fill the pond with the hose, the water's weight will force the liner into the shape of the hole. Fold any wrinkles caused by curved sides into neat pleats as the water rises. Trim off any surplus liner, leaving an overlap of 12in to be hidden by the edging. Form an overflow using plastic waste pipe leading to a bog garden or to a drain.

Edging

Formal ponds are usually bordered with tiles, slabs or flat stones. Use large pieces and let them overhang the edge of the pond by 2in, which will hide the liner above the surface of the water. Bed the slabs in a layer of wet 4:1 mix of mortar. Grout the joints the following day with a weak mortar mixture, brushing off surplus with a soft brush.

Planting

Grass is the best border for informal ponds. Either lay instant turf or sow seed, and cut grass regularly.

Herbaceous plants, such as *Hosta*, *Astilbe* and *Primula*, soften the edges of a new pond. Their reflection on the still water can be stunning and they will provide shade.

Keeping the pond clear

Sunlight reacts with minerals in the water to form a green algae. This, in turn, darkens the water, causing submerged plants to die from lack of light. To maintain a balance, shade a third of the surface of the pond using edging plants or large-leafed aquatics such as waterlilies. Stock the pond with oxygenating plants.

Child safety

You may need to put a fence around the pond until children are older. Or lay a galvanized grill, capable of supporting a child, over the water and hide it with smooth river cobbles. Strong fishing net, securely fastened, is less noticeable.

Edging materials should be non-slip. Check them regularly to make sure they haven't become loose.

How to build a patio

Every garden should have an area with a hard surface for entertaining or outdoor eating. Where better for a quiet snooze after a good meal? Originally, in Spain, a patio was a walled courtyard open to the sky. It was also the name for the floor where silver ores were amalgamated. While you may not aspire to a walled courtyard, there is still plenty of time to construct your own patio floor, or pay someone to provide one, before urgent jobs take precedence.

In our northern latitude, the sitting area should be in the sun. Morning sun is wonderful; sun in the evening is relaxing, and a south-facing patio will result in melted chocolate on the digestive biscuits. A north-facing patio is dreary, seldom used and prone to algae.

Size is important, though it will be dictated by cost, space and the numbers to be accommodated. When calculating the surface area, allow for garden furniture, including table and loungers. Where large garden parties are envisaged, an 'overflow' area, surfaced with gravel, will be quick and cheap to build. It may also double as a standing area for containers of summer bedding.

What you will need

- 2in quarry stone
- landscape fabric
- sand
- fine sand
- cement
- tiles
- plants
- compost

Tools

- spade
- shovel
- wheelbarrow
- compaction plate (hired)
- gloves
- safety boots
- timber straight edge
- pegs
- spirit level
- string
- soft brush
- trowel
- water supply

The foundation

Mark the shape and size of the patio using string, and then excavate, storing the topsoil for future use. Unless you intend landing a helicopter, the base need only be 6–8in deep. Use clean, 2in quarried stone, 4–6in deep. Vibrate and consolidate using a compaction plate (hired from a DIY outlet). It is hand held, simple to use, but heavy for loading and unloading.

Lay landscape fabric on top of the stone to prevent weeds, surface with 2in sand and vibrate. The finished level must be at least 6in below the damp-proof course of the house, and slightly sloping away to allow water to run off.

Drive in wooden pegs, using a spirit level and a straight-edged plank of wood to level. Slope the surface by placing a 1in block of wood under the spirit level on the lower side. Level by raising or lowering that peg until the bubble in the spirit level is centred. Keep the pegs evenly spaced and the fall will be uniform.

Surfaces

Choose a texture and colour to tie in with the surrounding walls. Ask to see a demonstration patio in the surface that interests you, rather than a few tiles. When using more than one material, check that they complement each other and are of the same thickness.

The main area needs to be even to accommodate table and chair legs. Granite setts and cobble stones form an irregular surface and are better used as an edge. Remember that materials of a consistent thickness will be easier to lay than reclaimed sandstone or slate, where the depth of each piece may vary. Choose a dry period to lay the patio; if it does rain, stop work and spread a cover.

Tiles, paviours, bricks and setts are laid on vibrated sand, butt-jointed with no gaps for grouting. The finished surface is brushed over with fine, dry sand and vibrated to fill the joints. Surplus sand is brushed off.

Slabs and crazy-paved materials are set on weak, dry mortar comprising four parts dry sand and one part (by volume) of cement. The mortar gradually absorbs moisture and sets. Grout the gaps with a slurry of mortar, brushing off the surplus the next day, using a soft brush to avoid leaving marks.

Steps

Make the steps as broad as possible – 4ft-plus will allow two people to walk together – and the lift or riser should be 6in. Each step should easily accommodate a size-10 shoe, and 18in wide is ideal. Allowing the steps to overhang by 2in will soften the look and hide part of the riser. If necessary, provide a handrail of shaped, galvanized tubing for safety, making sure it is well secured.

Planting

Leave a few small gaps around the perimeter of the patio, and make a planting hole excavating 10in of hardcore replacing it with gritty topsoil. Plant creepy-crawlies, such as thyme and *Helianthemum*, to sprawl over the surrounding surface.

Containers

The patio is most in demand during the summer, when plants need to look their best. They should be planted in containers which may be moved. Use pieces of broken clay pots or clean stones in the bottom of the container for drainage. The compost level should be 2in below the top of the container to allow for watering and topping up with fresh compost. Vibrant colours, fragrant flowers and aromatic foliage will be enjoyed, and if a plant with a hint of the Mediterranean can be included, the temperature will seem to rise.

Perfect patio plants

- *Agapanthus orientalis* is an evergreen perennial with broad, strap-shaped, dark-green leaves. In late summer and autumn, it produces rounded umbels of mid-blue flowers up to 12in across. Loves well-drained compost and sunny position. Grows to 24in high and prefers frost protection.
- Lavender, with its fragrant spikes of summer flowers and aromatic foliage, loves full sun. Try 'Munstead' with blue-purple flowers, 18in high.
- *Lilium regale* (regal lily). A bulb that grows to 5ft and has erect stems of narrow green leaves crowned with fragrant, trumpet-shaped, white flowers.
- Night-scented stock. A summer-flowering annual grown from seed or bought as young bedding plants. It produces masses of pink, purple or mauve flowers with a wonderful fragrance in the evening.
- *Perovskia* 'Blue Spire' is a shrub that enjoys a poor soil in full sun, producing 12in-long panicles of violet-blue flowers in summer, backed by silver-grey aromatic foliage.
- *Yucca filamentosa* (Adam's needle) has lance-shaped, dark evergreen leaves, margined with white threads, and upright panicles of white bell-shaped flowers in mid-summer.

Small trees

What could be better than a small ornamental tree on the south side of the patio to create a dappled corner? Three of the best are:

1. *Amelanchier lamarckii* (snowy mespilus). Round-headed deciduous tree with masses of white flowers in spring and a dazzling display of brilliant autumn leaf colour.
2. *Cotinus* 'Grace' (smoke tree). Deciduous, small tree or large shrub with wine-purple leaves in summer and plumes of purplish-pink flowers followed by orange-red autumn leaf colour.
3. *Sorbus vilmorinii* (Chinese rowan). Grows to 12ft, with deciduous, fern-like foliage and white flowers in spring, followed by clusters of small pink berries in autumn and winter.

How to protect plants in winter

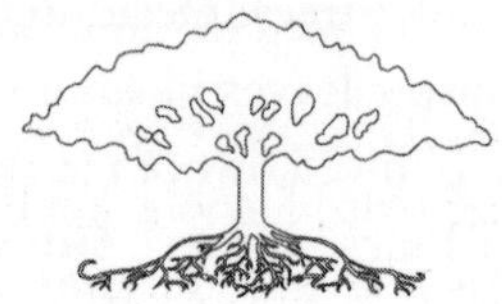

There are ways to keep young plants warm and dry, which do not involve the use of greenhouses. Cold frames, for instance, have been used for centuries to harden off young plants before they go out in spring and for winter protection.

Cloches are almost as old. They were originally fragile, cumbersome affairs made from panes of glass wired together. These days, a cloche can be fashioned from a sheet of rigid corrugated plastic; it is lightweight and easy to move.

Alternatively, polythene sheeting and wire hoops are used to make a 'continuous cloche' – a long, low tunnel.

A 'tunnel house' – high enough to stand up in – is basically a large, ventilated polythene cloche.

If you have a greenhouse, put the frame close by, making it easy to transfer plants that need hardening off before they are planted outside with no protection. A position in full sun is ideal.

Size and shape

A cold frame 6ft across and 4ft from front to back should be large enough for most gardens, allowing a decent-sized bed of compost or gravel. The frame should be 2ft at the back, sloping to 1ft at the front. The lid is made of rigid plastic or glass. It should be hinged at the back so that it can be opened.

Construction

Make the 'walls' of the cold frame from timber or brick. (Concrete blocks can be used, but the interior surfaces must be smoothly plastered to prevent pests hiding in the porous surface.) Fit angle iron on the sloping sides to hold the lid.

If you are making a wooden frame, use pressure-treated 1in-thick boards. Ensure that any preservative you paint on is plant-friendly.

You can fit a base made of wood, with holes drilled for drainage, inside the cold frame. Seed can be sown and cuttings rooted directly into a 6in layer of gritty compost laid over the base. Alternatively, if you do not fit a base, a 3in layer of washed gravel laid on landscape fabric will aid drainage and discourage weeds.

Using a cold frame

When the lid is propped open for ventilation, tie it with a length of cord to keep it secure. In the heat of summer, paint or spray the glass with shading to prevent the sun scorching the foliage. Insulate the frame in winter by lining the inside of the lid with plastic bubble wrap.

Making a cloche

The traditional cloche, made from sheets of glass, was shaped either like a tent, or like a Dutch barn (with a shallow-sloping 'roof' and steeper 'walls').

Rigid corrugated plastic can be used in exactly the same way simply by creasing a single sheet into the desired shape. Peg the cloche over the crop by pushing U-shaped pieces of wire through the sides and into the ground. For ease of weeding the pots, watering and working with plants, cut a flap in one side of the sloping roof. Wedged open, this will also allow air to circulate.

Wash the cloche frequently: green algae and splashes of mud will reduce the amount of daylight reaching the plants.

Place the cloche over the plot one week before you use it, to allow the soil to warm up.

Tunnels

'Walk-in' tunnel house kits are available from 8ft to 20ft wide, and from 20ft to over 100ft in length. Wide tunnels allow more height for growing tall crops. Find a length and width to suit your growing needs.

Site

A tunnel is not as attractive a structure as a greenhouse and should be sited in the least obvious position. It should be well clear of overhanging trees, which cause algae to grow on the tunnel. A level, well-drained area of grass is ideal.

Avoid ground that has been overcultivated for a long time, as the soil will be short of nutrients and there is a good chance that it may have been contaminated with pests and diseases. A tap inside the tunnel will make watering much easier.

Materials

All the necessary materials are supplied in the kit, including foundation tubes, 1in diameter, galvanized-steel tube hoops, and brace and ridge tubes.

The polythene cover is normally of 720g thickness and usually has a four-year guarantee. Thermal or 'anti-fog' sheeting is of the same thickness, but is specially treated to limit condensation on the inside and reduce heat loss. As an extra, order rolls of 'anti-hotspot' tape. It will prolong the life of the cover by acting as a buffer between the hot metalwork and the polythene, preventing chafing. With smaller tunnels, the entrance is covered with a roll-up door of polythene and wooden laths.

You will need

Spirit level, string, tape measure, sledgehammer, spade, hammer, saw, wheelbarrow, Stanley knife.

Construction

Line out the two sides of the polytunnel with parallel strings. Mark where the hoops will go, keeping them at right angles to the string and spacing them an equal distance apart. Drive the foundation tubes (the short, thicker, metal tubes) into the ground, keeping them vertical and making sure each stands the same height above ground. If the ground is soft or stony, dig a hole 1in square and 6in deep for each tube and concrete them in place. Keep the top of the concrete 1in below soil level. Leave it for a few days to harden.

Four inches out from the foundation tubes, dig a trench 9in deep and 12in wide, throwing the soil to the outside of the trench.

Fit the two halves of the hoops together and slide the ends into the foundation tubes. Clip on the brace and ridge tubes to hold the framework steady. Apply the anti-hotspot tape to pad the connections.

This is a good stage at which to cultivate the ground without being hindered by the cover. Dig in compost and lay the path.

With as many helping hands as possible, slide the cover over the hoops starting at one end. Stretch the cover as tightly as possible, then bury the surplus in the trench. Back-fill the trenches with ½in round river gravel. To allow rainwater running off the roof to seep away, use a digging fork to puncture the cover every few feet in the bottom of the trench.

The door is made from surplus polythene stretched over a frame made from 3in×2in planed wood. The doorframe is made from two timber uprights concreted into the ground, made rigid with a crossbeam at the top.

With smaller houses, a roll-up 'blind' is used instead of a door. Fashion two uprights for a 'doorframe': each is made from two 2in×1in wooden battens, joined only at the top and the bottom by being screwed to a 2in-thick wooden spacer. Take a sheet of polythene 6in wider than the opening, and to it tack (roughly 12in apart) horizontal laths of 1in×1in timber, each also 6in wider than the opening. These laths will slide up and down inside the uprights. The top of the 'blind' is tacked to the crossbar above the opening.

How to put up a greenhouse

The greenhouse is no longer a luxury. Indeed, no gardener should be without one – and those who are probably know exactly what they are missing. But it is not hard to fill the gap in your life: greenhouses of all shapes and sizes are available as DIY kits, either by mail order or from garden centres.

The framework is made from wood or aluminium alloy, each of which has its advantages and disadvantages. Metal is cheaper and does not need to be painted or treated, but wood is more attractive and loses less heat at night.

Site

Planning permission is not usually necessary for small or medium-sized structures, but there are exceptions, so it is best to check. Advising your neighbours of your plans may prevent friction.

Place the structure well away from trees and tall hedges in an open, sunny, level situation sheltered from strong winds. It will cost less to install electricity and water if the site is close to the house. Avoid areas that are in a frost pocket.

The soil should be free-draining and not part of the vegetable garden. Soils that have been cropped for years should be dug out and replaced with fresh, loamy soil.

Orientation

Some people site rectangular greenhouses with the ridge of the roof running from east to west, but I prefer the long sides to face east and west, allowing in more light in morning and evening. Place the door facing away from the coldest, windiest side. If you are designing a lean-to structure, build it against a west-facing wall. Walls facing south are too hot in summer.

Foundations

Greenhouses up to 8ft x 6ft are normally bolted on to concrete plinths or kerbs bought with the greenhouse. Larger structures will need a concrete foundation. Some greenhouses are raised on 3ft-high brick walls. These will require foundations 18in deep to carry the extra weight.

Make sure the site is level. Mark the exact location of each wall using a line stretched between wooden pegs. Make sure all the corners are 90 degrees. Dig foundation trenches 9in wide and 9in deep, keeping the line that marks the wall in the centre of the trench. Fill with well-firmed concrete and smooth the surface with a plastering trowel.

Assembly

There are people who are born to assemble alloy greenhouses, but I am not one of them. It is theoretically an elementary task and I can manage it, but it takes me for ever. Most outlets offer an erection service – if in doubt, make use of it.

The base of the greenhouse must be drilled and bolted to the plinth. Timber-framed greenhouses are delivered as unglazed sections: four sides, plus the roof in two parts. Providing you have help, the sections bolt together easily, forming a strong structure.

Try to glaze the house in one day, or an overnight wind may cause damage. When the glazing is done, check that the glazing bars are parallel and that the house as a whole is not lopsided.

When handling glass, always wear strong gloves. The sheets should overlap to keep out rainwater. To prevent a build-up of dirt and algae, the upper pane should overhang by no more than half an inch.

Ventilation

Choose a greenhouse with as many ventilators as possible. It is essential to have side vents as well as roof openings, to encourage the movement of air. If there aren't any, remove a pane of glass in each side and fit a cover of fine mesh net to keep out birds and animals.

Finishing

Fit a gutter and downpipe to each long side of the greenhouse and collect rainwater in a water butt with a run-off tap at the base.

Though not essential, mains electricity is the cleanest and simplest way of providing heat and light. Arrange for a professional electrician to install the supply. All power points must be water-proofed; fit an RCD circuit-breaker to each piece of electrical equipment.

How to build pergolas, trellises and arbours

Timber is at home in the garden. It looks natural and blends in so well that some gardeners have taken to staining it blue to make it noticeable.

Wooden pergolas and arbours provide interest, as well as a framework for climbing plants and a shelter from the elements. They add solid height to the garden in a different way from trees. Trellis fencing helps to separate garden rooms and ensures privacy, while timber rafters, supported on upright posts or classical columns, provide the means for climbers to scramble across, 'roofing' the pergola and offering some protection from the weather.

What you will need

- timber impregnated under pressure with preservative

- galvanized fixing-spikes or concrete
- galvanized nails
- galvanized U-shaped brackets

Tools

- saw
- hammer
- spirit level
- spade
- shovel
- sledgehammer
- wheelbarrow

Where

Site the pergola where it will not stand in isolation. If it is near tall shrubs, they will appear to reduce the height. Do not construct it where it is in permanent shade.

Your pergola may be built against a wall of the house where there is an existing door giving direct access to a room. It then becomes an extension of your house.

Wherever you site it, try to connect the pergola to the house with a path. At least one open side should face south or east so that it receives sun for most of the day.

Design

The pergola should blend into your garden and, rather than being purely ornamental, become a place to entertain and relax. Where it is constructed to enclose a path, leave adequate space on either side to accommodate climbing plants. The sides are a useful vertical screen for climbers.

Construction

The main uprights should be set in concrete or secured with a fixing spike driven into the ground. Where the pergola is being constructed on a solid paved surface, use metal post-fixing plates, which are bolted to the paviours to hold the uprights.

Check the posts are vertical with a spirit level. Solid-looking, 8in x 6in corner posts give an impression of permanency. Roofing rafters should be strong enough to support your weight and are usually 6in x 3in. To prevent the roof timbers moving, they may be notched into the cross members. Alternatively, galvanized U-brackets can be attached to the cross beams. The rafters are firmly held by the brackets. To prevent rusting, use galvanized nails.

Extend the roof timbers 9–12in beyond the cross members and bevel the ends. Make the cut on the underside so that the exposed timber-grain is protected.

Galvanized netting wire or fine-mesh plastic netting fixed to the rafters allows plants to grip and scramble over the roof without the need for constant training and tying.

Lattice trellis-panels are ideal for the sides of the pergola. To avoid a boxed-in feel, make some of the panels different heights, with gaps at the bottom or the top.

Gazebos and arbours

Gazebos and arbours are available in kit form ready for erection. Visit a builder's merchant or fencing manufacturer for a selection of trellis and latticework panels that will give the 'room' character.

Trellis screen

Fencing makes a wonderful boundary for privacy and shelter. It is useful for separating different styles of planting and, draped with climbers, it adds colour and fragrance.

Rustic screens, constructed from natural wood, with or without the bark removed, give a rural look. As the timber dries out, bark tends to peel. Ask for pressure-treated timber. The uprights are usually 3in in diameter and are sold as standard 8ft lengths. Construct the fence on site, concreting the uprights into the ground 6ft apart. Use a cord to keep them in a straight line and at the same height. Use sufficient lengths of 2in-diameter poles to form a decorative pattern. Where more than one panel is needed, they should be made to the same design.

Cut ends of timber should be soaked in preservative, or at least painted, to prevent rotting. Use a treatment that is not detrimental to plants.

Timber arches may be made in the same way with a pair of uprights, set well back, on each side of the path. The roof of the arch may be pitched or flat providing it is sufficiently above head height to accommodate thorny climbing roses.

Wall trellis

Attached to a wall, wooden trellis-panels make attractive supports for climbing plants. Use 1in wooden spacers between the trellis and the wall to allow the stems to twine round the frame. Walls that need to be painted on a regular basis are a problem if there are plants. Hinge the bottom of the trellis panel to the wall and hold the top in place with a hook that allows the panel, plant and all, to be lowered to the ground and lifted up again when the paint is dry. Fruit trees may be planted and trained to cover the framework. Climbing and twining plants, such as roses and honeysuckle, require support. Other free-standing shrubs may be planted if they have a framework to be trained against.

Planting

The planting area should be well prepared. Dig a hole at least twice as large as the plant root ball. Add lots of old farmyard manure or compost; a handful of bone meal mixed into the soil, as it is being firmed round the roots, also helps.

Water in the plant to settle the soil round the roots. Mulch the surface of the soil to prevent it drying out in the warmer summer months.

Tie the plant to the support until it takes hold. Evergreen climbers give year-round shelter and interest, and *Clematis armandii*, with its long, leathery leaves and white scented flowers in early spring, is ideal for training over the roof of an arbour.

Wisteria needs careful pruning to ensure long, trailing flowers. Peaches, nectarines and vines can be trained and tied to a trellis, producing fruit outdoors in all but the most exposed sites.

Shrubs, including the evergreen *Pyracantha* with its yellow, orange or red berries and *Cytisus battandieri*, the pineapple broom, may be trained and tied to a wooden frame. Tie the shoots with twine or raffia that will not cut into the soft stems. Where wires are used, check them each season and slacken as necessary to avoid choking the plants as they mature. Plant scented varieties around the sitting area.

Ideal plants for a pergola or trellis

- *Akebia quinata* is a vigorous, twining, semi-evergreen climber with deep-green leaves, blue-green on the underside. The small vanilla-scented, maroon-chocolate flowers appear in late spring and, in a hot summer, are followed by purple sausage-shaped fruit. Likes a well-drained, fertile soil.
- *Campsis × tagliabuana* 'Madame Galen' is deciduous with dark-green divided leaves. The beautiful apricot-pink trumpet-shaped flowers hang in clusters in late summer and autumn. Does best in a sheltered, sunny site.
- Clematis. My favourite is *C.* 'Proteus'. Deciduous and not too vigorous, it produces large double mauve-pink flowers with light-pink centres. It prefers a site in semi-shade.
- *Humulus lupulus* 'Aureus' (hops) is a herbaceous, twining climber with lime-green to yellow leaves. The small greenish-yellow hops are papery and cone-like. Prefers a sunny, well-drained position.
- *Jasminum officinale* f. *affine*. A twining, semi-evergreen climber with dark-green leaves and clusters of fragrant, tubular pink flowers that open to white. Best in full sun.
- *Lonicera japonica* 'Halliana' (honeysuckle). Semi-evergreen, twining climber with bright green leaves and fragrant white flowers. Prefers a well-drained soil.
- Climbing rose. For reliability it is hard to beat 'Compassion': a large-flowered climber with pink-flushed yellow blooms.
- *Vitis coignetiae* (crimson glory vine). A strong-growing, deciduous, tendril climber with dark-green leaves. The pale-green flowers produce bunches of tiny black grapes in autumn. Prefers an alkaline, well-drained soil.

How to build a cascade or fountain

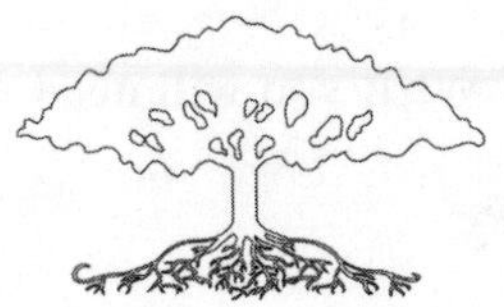

Fountains

Most submersible pumps are sold complete with a small fountain kit and a selection of heads to form different patterns of water. The flow may be adjusted.

The pool needs to be large enough to contain spray drift from the fountain on a windy day. If there is water loss, it will need constant topping up.

Elaborate sculptures require careful positioning. Large, heavy fountains can damage pre-formed and flexible liners, and should only be placed in pools with a concrete base that can support the weight.

Waterfalls and cascades

It is possible to have more than one water feature by fitting a T-pipe to the pump outlet. Where a large-volume waterfall is required, the bulk of the water should be directed through a larger-diameter hose with less being directed to the fountain.

By raising the top outlet high above the pump, you reduce the flow of water.

In most gardens, a 6–8ft-high feature is sufficient to provide a spectacular cascade and waterfall with a sound to match.

What you will need

- submersible pump
- electricity supply
- RCD circuit-breaker
- hose
- liner or pre-moulded cascade
- cement
- sand

Tools

- knife
- screwdriver
- jubilee clips
- pointing trowel
- spirit level

Safety

Engage a qualified electrician for all electrical work. Use armoured cable and waterproof connectors, and join to the power via a circuit-breaker.

How to move water

A pump will let you operate a fountain or have a cascade of water with a waterfall. The pump circulates the pool water, so you do not need mains water. Submersible pumps are popular, being silent and inconspicuous. Position the pump in the deepest part of the pond, raised on bricks to keep it above any sediment. Camouflage the electric cable and hoses with stones or marginal plants. The motor draws water in through a filter, which traps leaves, debris and algae and forces the water out, under pressure, through the hose or directly to the fountain.

Filtering

Clean the filter every few days when the pump is running. The need for additional filters will depend on the ecological balance of the pool. A combination of plants and wildlife will keep the water clear, preventing algae or green water from forming.

With a biological system, the water passes through filters containing beneficial bacteria that convert harmful nitrites into useful nitrates.

If the water turns pea green with algae, an ultra-violet box may be incorporated into the delivery system, the light from which will break down the algae.

Both these systems are outside the pool and need to be camouflaged with rocks or plants.

Construction

Build a rockery nearby. Run a length of reinforced hose from the pump to the top of the rockery, burying it in the soil and under the rocks to keep it from freezing in winter. Lay a strip of flexible liner, on sand, down the side of the rockery facing the pool. Build in a bend and make some deeper areas to retain water when the pump is switched off. Birds will use these for bathing. The sides of the cascade are built up with rock high enough to hold the water and hide the liner. The floor may be covered with small stones and gravel. At the base, let the water shoot over a flat rock into the pool.

The rate of flow affects the sound and may be changed by placing small rocks in the path of the water. The bigger the drop from the waterfall, the louder the splash. Allow the cascade liner to overhang the side of the pool so that water lost on the way down flows back in. Where space allows, keep the rockery back from the pool edge so that the waterfall can flow into a river constructed in the same way as the cascade.

Maintenance

Pinhole outlets are easily blocked by fine debris. Clearing the hole from the outside allows the blockage to reappear at another outlet. Instead, remove the head of the fountain and turn the pump on, washing out the debris. Also clean the filter if necessary.

When water freezes, it expands sufficiently to crack plastic and stone. As a precaution, drain the system in the winter. In summer, regularly top up the level to replace evaporated water. If a lot of mains water is added at one time, the natural balance may be upset, causing the water to discolour.

Plants and planting

Waterlilies dislike moving water and do not tolerate spray from fountains, so need to be positioned well away from waterfalls. Choose varieties that are suitable for the depth of water. Plant labels refer to the distance from the surface to the top of the plant basket.

Submerged and oxygenating plants have the ability to choke a pool and should be vigorously thinned out every year. To prevent blocking the filter, switch off the pump before you start and do not run it until the debris has settled below the pump filter.

Marginals such as *Caltha palustrus* 'Flore Pleno', the yellow, double-flowering marsh marigold, and *Houttuynia cordata* 'Chameleon', that has leaves splashed with cream, yellow, red and green, are happy growing with their roots in shallow water or damp soil along the bank. They do not mind moving water, providing the soil is not washed from around their roots. Use small rocks to form pockets where the soil will be stable.

Ferns are ideal for overhanging a cascade and their fronds can trail in the water, hiding any areas of liner not disguised by rock. Plants that cast shade on part of the water will help prevent algae forming. Large-leafed *Hostas*, such as *Hosta* 'Big Daddy' and *Rodgersia podophylla*, planted on the south side of the pool, will throw good reflections. *Juniperus* 'Pfitzeriana Aurea', with its golden-green evergreen foliage, throws out branches that are almost horizontal. They provide shade and hide fish from the beady eyes of hungry herons.

How to build a rockery

Building your own rockery is an enjoyable activity, offering tremendous satisfaction when the final rock completes a mountain scene in miniature. Choose plants that will be in keeping with the scale of your rockery. Avoid fast-growing shrubs and rampant perennials, which will swamp the rocks they are meant to nestle among.

The two main ingredients are rock and soil. Naturally weathered rocks are sold at garden centres, but they tend to be smaller than those from your local quarry. Larger rocks are more difficult to move, but will give a more realistic miniature cliff or outcrop. All the rocks should be of a single type – such as slate or sandstone.

Take care to get hold of topsoil that is free of perennial weed roots. Since most alpine plants dislike heavy, wet conditions, a free-draining, gravelly soil is ideal.

What you will need

- topsoil
- coarse grit
- rocks
- 13mm gravel to match the rocks
- plants

Tools

- spade
- shovel
- wheelbarrow
- crowbar
- hand trowel
- gloves
- safety boots

Site

Decide on an area free from shade for most of the day and clear of overhanging trees. If a gently sloping bank is available, cut into it to set the rocks. Mark out a flat area using string, sand or a length of hosepipe and strip any grass or weeds, digging deep to remove all perennial weed roots. Remember a large rockery requires large quantities of rock. This will cost a great deal of time and money.

Safety

Wear gloves and safety boots when handling rocks. Make sure you have a firm grip and keep your back straight by bending your knees.

Bedding each rock in concrete will prevent accidents when you are maintaining the rockery.

Construction

On a flat site, the bottom layer of rocks should be partly buried. Angle each rock with its front edge higher than the back so it appears to 'grow' out of the soil. Rainwater will run down the top of the rock into the soil. Before placing each rock, examine its shape and keep the most interesting to the front and top. If there are strata lines – common in sandstone – ensure that the lines run horizontally.

A crowbar is useful for levering rocks into position without fingers being trapped. Small pieces of stone can be used to level the rocks, but gaps should be back-filled with firmed-down soil.

The second tier is laid with the front of each rock resting on the back of the one below. Where you want to create a pocket of soil, set a piece farther back than the one beneath it.

A free-standing rockery will look more natural if it isn't built in the shape of a pyramid. Build one side as a steep cliff, with the other sloping down.

A well-drained, impoverished, gravelly soil is ideal for building on. The soil you use for planting should be a mixture of weed-free topsoil with an equal bulk of grit or fine gravel, plus half the amount of a peat substitute or old compost – but no fertilizer.

Use a dibber or a hand trowel to make sure the crevices are well filled. Finally, brush off any surplus soil, hose the rocks clean and water to help settle the soil.

Scree

To create a scree-like effect, cover part of the rockery with a gravel that matches the stone. If larger rocks are partly buried, small mat-forming plants can be encouraged to grow over them. The scree bed could be extended to become a gravel path.

Rock garden plants

There are two main groups of plants (excluding dwarf conifers and shrubs) that are used in rock gardens.

Alpine plants grow above the tree line in mountain ranges and can tolerate low temperatures and cold winds. They are low-growing and generally flower in spring to allow seed to form, ripen and scatter before winter sets in. They prefer to be planted in full sun and their foliage suffers if kept wet for a long time. Deep roots anchor the plant and search out water.

Rockery plants are small, slow-growing plants suitable for confined, well-drained, sunny sites. They are easier to grow than alpines and their flowers will provide colour well into the summer.

Planting tips

In cold, exposed areas, get young plants off to a good start by planting in spring. Don't plant large specimens for instant effect – they will be difficult to squeeze into the pockets of soil and may not thrive as well as a smaller plant. Plant firmly, without fertilizer, with the roots at the same depth as they were in the pot or their previous position. A layer of coarse grit or chippings will act as a mulch and helps keep down weeds.

Space

Some plants, particularly rock plants such as *Helianthemum* (rock rose), are low-growing but spread to cover rocks.

Root run

Many alpines require a deep, free-draining soil that allows roots to seek water.

Soil type

Both alpine and rock plants need a well-drained, moisture-retentive soil, but some require alkalinity soil, while others will succeed only in acid conditions. For example, *Gentiana sino-ornata*, the autumn gentian – a semi-evergreen – prefers an acid soil, while its cousin *Gentiana verna*, the star gentian – evergreen, with sky-blue spring flowers – needs a neutral or alkaline soil.

Special needs

Verbascum dumulosum, with its felted, greyish evergreen foliage, dislikes our wet winters. Plant it in a freely drained alkaline soil with a rock overhang for protection, or on its side in a vertical crevice between two rocks. *Lewisia cotyledon* hybrids, which have rosettes of thick, fleshy evergreen leaves, should be planted in the same way.

Flowering time and colour

Alpines flower early in the year, so to extend the rockery's colour through to autumn, include rock plants and even dwarf bulbs.

Best varieties

- *Aquilegia formosa*: orange-red flowers in late spring and early summer. Likes a rich, well-drained soil. Self-sows. Height 24in, spread 18in.

- Dalmatian bellflower (*Campanula portenschlagiana*): evergreen with bell-shaped, deep-purple flowers in summer. Height 8in, spread 24in.
- New Zealand daisy (*Celmisia walkeri*): evergreen with large white daisy flowers in early summer. Prefers a well-drained acid soil. Height and spread 12in.
- *Daphne arbuscula*: evergreen shrub with fragrant pink flowers in late spring and early summer. Height 6in, spread 18in.
- Cheddar pink (*Dianthus gratianopolitanus*): evergreen with deep pink, fragrant flowers in summer. Height 6in, spread 18in.
- Welsh poppy (*Meconopsis cambrica*): semi-evergreen with yellow-to-orange single flowers from spring to autumn. Likes a well-drained soil. Height 18in, spread 12in.
- Red admiral (*Phlox douglasii*): evergreen with deep-crimson flowers in late spring and early summer. Height 9in, spread 12in.
- Hallen's pasque flower (*Pulsatilla halleri*): goblet-shaped, violet flowers in late spring. Height 9in, spread 8in.
- *Saxifraga* 'Tumbling Waters': evergreen with small white flowers in spring. Height 16in, spread 9in.
- English violet (*Viola odorata*): semi-evergreen with sweet-scented purple or white flowers in late winter and spring. Height 8in, spread 12in.

How to build a rock garden

A well-constructed rockery will add height to an otherwise flat garden; at the same time, it can help to deal with a potential problem area such as a boggy spot or depression that is difficult to incorporate into the garden. It brings a new dimension to the space, allowing you to grow little gems such as *Lewisia cotyledon* hybrids that are difficult to place elsewhere.

When deciding where to put your rockery, choose a position in full sun and not directly under leafy trees. Building up the soil will allow you to rise above nasty, sticky clay, limey soil or areas with poor drainage. Ideally, the site should be free of perennial weeds, but it is possible to protect against most types.

Materials

You will need to order soil, rocks, grit and gravel, which can be delivered to your front door ready for an early start on Saturday morning. At lunchtime, take a break and visit the garden centre with your plant list.

The topsoil you buy must be weed-free. Check the source. You don't want to buy in weeds, pests and diseases from some derelict garden that is being stripped of soil. It must be an open, free-draining soil. Some of the rocks should be as large as you can handle. Round boulders are difficult to lay and never look natural. All the rocks should be of the same type. Basalt, granite, sandstone or limestone are ideal, especially if the pieces are weathered. Where there are strata lines running through sandstone, all the pieces must run in the same direction: if some are horizontal and others vertical, they will look a shambles.

The grit will be used as a mulch and the gravel will form the scree bed. Both should be bought ready-washed to eliminate dirt and sand. I prefer the colours to match; if you are going to try to recreate a mountain in miniature, the grit and gravel should be similar in tone to the rock.

Tools

Essential equipment includes a wheelbarrow, shovel, planting trowel, crowbar, strong gloves and boots with steel toecaps. A sledgehammer isn't essential, but may come in handy.

Construction

Once you have decided on the position of the rockery, lay a sheet of landscape fabric on the site to prevent perennial weeds contaminating the new soil. This is also a good opportunity to hide unwanted hardcore. A layer of broken slabs, old patio tiles, bricks and lumps of concrete will help drainage and reduce the need for expensive topsoil.

Pile the topsoil into a mound, making sure there is at least 12in over the debris. Shape the heap so it has at least one gently sloping side that can act as a scree area. If it is to be cone-shaped, the top should be flat.

Start placing the rocks from the bottom up. Each piece should be set into the soil rather than on top of it. Make a firm bed and place the rock with a flat side on the soil. The top should slope slightly to the rear to make it steady and allow rain to run off the surface towards the plants. Use the crowbar to lever large rocks into place.

Position the rocks close together with small spaces between the ends. These vertical cracks can be filled with soil and planted with rosette-leafed plants such as *Lewisia*. This prevents rain lying in the heart of the plant and causing the leaves to rot.

Where space allows, place one rock on top of the one below, like a step. There are lots of rock-hugging plants that will enjoy tumbling over the stone to carpet and follow the shape. The idea is to leave pockets of soil bounded by rocks rather than lots of soil with a few lumps of rock. Otherwise it would be a soilery.

Check if it looks natural. If a rock looks out of place, move it until it looks right. Cover the soil with a 2in layer of clean grit. Planting through this will help surface drainage and prevent the collar of the plant rotting during winter. It will also act as a mulch, reducing weeds. Dig a few holes in the slope and bury rocks, leaving a small portion exposed. Cover the slope with the gravel, allowing the rocks to peek out as they would on an alpine slope. The job is now finished and ready for planting.

How to make paths

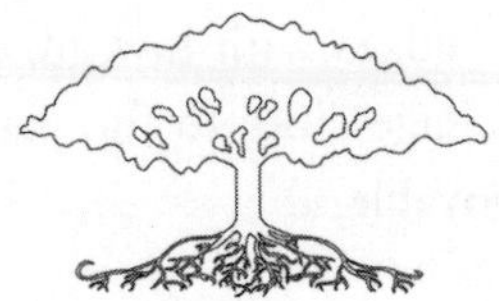

Paths are the backbone of a garden. Curved paths, meandering like a stream, can be used to show off highlights, while the straight paths of a formal garden are a joy to push a wheelbarrow along. But any path must lead somewhere, even if it's just to a shed or a seat.

A path less than 24in wide is uncomfortable for strolling on, and, if space permits, you should make it wide enough for two people to walk abreast. Run your path close to shrubs, but not so close that they need constant cutting back.

A path across a lawn should be laid with its surface slightly below the roots of the grass to prevent damage to a lawnmower.

Decide on a material before you start: its thickness will determine how deep you must dig. Paviours and tiles of every shape, size and colour are available, priced from about £10 per sq/m to 'don't walk on those, they cost the earth'. Crazy paving and brick are fashionable again, but if you are laying bricks in repeating patterns, remember that a complicated design will be slow to lay.

Gravel paths are non-slip, but must be edged to stop the gravel escaping. Keep the surface lower than the grass and edge with 2in-thick treated timber.

Round-topped concrete garden kerbs are also good for edging a path, as are kerb setts, bricks and reproduction Victorian rope edging. Finally, soften the edges with low-growing plants. Aromatic flowers and scented foliage close to the path will make strolling along it even more enjoyable.

What you will need

- hardcore
- sand
- cement
- tiles
- slabs
- bricks or gravel

Tools

- straight-edge
- spirit level
- wheelbarrow
- aerosol marker
- compaction plate (which can be hired)
- power stone-cutter (again, hired)
- pointing trowel
- soft brush

Excavation

Mark out the path with a line, hose or aerosol marker. The sides must be parallel and the width must remain constant. Remove top-soil for use elsewhere. Grass sods, stacked grass side down, will rot, adding humus to the soil heap – useful as potting compost or for the greenhouse.

Excavate to a depth that allows for 4in of hardcore and sand plus the thickness of the finished surface.

Edging

Fasten timber edging with galvanized nails to wooden pegs set in the ground at 6ft intervals. Bed hard edging, such as bricks or kerbs, in concrete.

Foundation

Spread 1–2in clean quarry stone 3in deep and settle with a compaction plate. Top up with compacted sand.

Laying the path

Tiles for walker and wheelbarrow use may be laid on sand. However, if mini-tractors and heavy machinery such as rotavators are using the path, the slabs should be bedded in a mix of five parts sand and one part (by volume) of cement. Mix well, then add enough water to make it supple (a little plasticizer in the water will keep the mortar workable for longer).

Small tiles, bricks and setts are usually laid close together with no gaps between. Fine sand is brushed over the surface and vibrated into the cracks with a compaction plate. Larger slabs are laid with a $^1/_4$in gap all round and grouted with a mix of three parts soft sand to one part cement. To avoid stains, apply the grout as a dry mix: water the gaps with a hose, let the surface dry, then brush the dry mortar into the gaps with a soft brush. Don't walk on it for a few days to let the mortar set.

Keeping the curve

Crazy paving is easily laid in a curved path, but big, straight-sided slabs must be cut with a power saw so they fit together, or laid leaving a wedge-shaped gap. An unusual effect is to cobble these gaps with round river stones of 1–2in diameter. Bed them in soft mortar (edged with timber until it sets) and tap them level with a straight-edge.

Edging plants

- Lavender (*Lavandula angustifolia*) with its aromatic, grey-green foliage makes a wonderful low hedge. Try 'Hidcote'. Plant 12in apart in a sunny, well-drained soil. Cotton lavender (*Santolina chamaecyparissus*) is another good aromatic shrub for hedging. Plant 10in apart in well-drained soil and clip lightly after flowering.
- Box (*Buxus sempervirens* 'Suffruticosa') makes a classic, formal, dwarf hedge. With regular clipping it can be kept to a height of 6in. Plant 10in apart.
- Heathers, especially varieties of *Erica carnea*, which flower in winter and tolerate alkaline soils, are perfect for narrow borders. *Erica* 'December Red', with dark leaves and rosy-red, late-winter flowers, grows in a hummock 8in high. Clip off dead spikes after flowering for a bushier plant.

- Shrubby wallflower (*Erysimum* 'Bowles's Mauve') is an evergreen perennial with greyish leaves that forms a 24in mound. Its mauve flowers are produced from mid-winter to summer. In mild areas some flowers will be present for most of the year.
- *Dianthus* 'Mrs Sinkins' is an old-fashioned pink with strongly scented white, double, fringed flowers. It likes well-drained alkaline soil. Mix with other clove-scented varieties for a low border of summer colour.
- Lemon thyme (*Thymus* × *citriodorus*) is evergreen with lemon-scented leaves and deep-pink flowers in summer. Plant in a sunny, dry soil and clip lightly after flowering. It grows to 12in.

PART II
Plants

Garden hedges that won't upset the neighbours

I feel sorry for the Leyland cypress. It is certainly ubiquitous and is the cause of much acrimony and worse – but it isn't its fault. It should carry a government health warning or, better still, a label pointing out that it is fast-growing and that its ultimate height is more than 100ft with a spread exceeding 30ft.

Leylandii are reasonably well behaved when they are regularly trimmed and maintained at a sensible height. The problem lies in their habit of growth. The evergreen foliage is only a shell. Within the green skin the plant is a mass of bare stems that will never in the future have foliage. This means that you can't reduce the width. They may be severely topped, but the growth will quickly be replaced with more of the same.

Mixed shrubs

But without *leylandii*, what is there to fill the gaps if you are after something quick-growing, evergreen and offering privacy and shelter? The answer is a row of tall mixed shrubs. These would be an asset viewed from either side of the fence. Be sensitive when pruning: much of their beauty would be lost if they were constantly cut to a standard height.

There are loads of great varieties suitable for acid soil, including the evergreen camellias that may be purchased as large plants. Avoid east-facing sites where a spring frost, followed by early morning sun, can destroy their flowers. *Camellia × williamsii* varieties, such as 'Donation' (semi-double pink), 'Anticipation' (large, double crimson) and 'St Ewe' (single, rose-pink) are quick-growing and flower well as young plants. Stems that are reaching for the sky may be cut back in early summer. Both *Pieris floribunda* and *Desfontainia spinosa* enjoy an acid soil and are evergreen.

The latter has glossy, dark-green, holly-like leaves with yellow-tipped, red flowers in summer and early autumn.

The leaves of *Pieris floribunda* remain dark green without any colouring but it produces masses of upright panicles of pure white flowers in early spring. Another variety, *P.* 'Beth Chandler' makes a good display with its pink leaves turning creamy-yellow and then dark green. And it occasionally produces small white flowers in late spring.

Evergreens and conifers

You can't be fined for growing spiky plants and a first class, evergreen barrier is furze (gorse). The secret of success is to grow the non-seeding variety, *Ulex europaeus* 'Flore Pleno'. Its pea-like, coconut-scented, bright-yellow flowers are double, appearing throughout the year. As fellow *Gardeners' Question Time* panellist Bob Flowerdew says: 'When gorse is out of flower, love is out of fashion.' It will seldom grow above 6ft but is tolerant of hard pruning, which will rejuvenate an old plant.

Viburnum japonicum is the only evergreen viburnum that is content to behave itself at about 6ft. Clusters of small, white, fragrant flowers appear in early summer followed by bright-red berries in the autumn.

I can think of no quick-growing conifers that will stop at the 6ft mark. You could invest in specimen plants, such as the golden Irish yew, *Taxus baccata* 'Fastigiata Aureomarginata' with its small, evergreen leaves margined in bright yellow. Being columnar and slow-growing it is easily maintained by clipping at a suitable height, but in my view the practice is nothing short of cruel. The dwarf variety *T.b.* 'Standishii' is a female selection of the Irish yew with golden-yellow foliage, which will slowly reach a height of about 6ft.

Formal or informal?

Formal hedges may be maintained at an agreeable height and there are many desirable plants to provide an aesthetically attractive screen. For instance, beech with its retained brown, winter leaves and new, light-green foliage has many admirers. Others prefer variegated holly, which forms a dense green and gold screen but requires twice yearly clipping.

Informal, flowering hedges are good value for money. *Escallonia* has attractive, glossy, evergreen leaves and panicles of flowers all summer. There are white-, pink-, red- and crimson-flowered varieties. Evergreen berberis include *B.* × *stenophylla* with tiny, dark-green, spine-tipped leaves, and lemon-yellow spring flowers on long arching branches. In late summer these branches are laden with blue-black fruit.

How to plant

These long-term shrubs deserve the best of attention at planting time.

- Where they are replacing large plants that have been removed, the soil will be exhausted of nutrients.
- Enrich it with the main elements of nitrogen, phosphate and potash.
- Digging in lots of old, well-rotted farmyard manure and compost will bulk up the humus content, making the soil more moisture retentive.
- Remove as many of the previous occupant's roots as possible. They are difficult to work around and may encourage diseases such as honey fungus.
- Large, container-grown specimens may require a stake, especially if they are providing shelter by filling a windy gap.
- A deep mulch of compost or shredded bark will finish the job.

The Law

Undoubtedly the *leylandii's* speed of growth and heavy, dense, evergreen foliage have played a part in its downfall. But under the new two-metre law, slow-growing evergreens are also in the firing line.

Gardeners and garden designers will have to rethink their choice of evergreen shrubs. Most of my neighbours are cows and sheep – and a good job, too.

I have mixed shrubberies with *Escallonia* 'Iveyi', *Choisya ternata*, *Berberis stenophylla* and *Viburnum rhytidophyllum* and many other excellent, almost essential, evergreens, all of which stand at between 10ft and 13ft in height.

However, there are species of these shrubs that will only grow approximately to the specified two metres. To have to prune other shrubs annually to conform to the height restriction will be a nuisance and some will retain a chopped appearance long after pruning.

Bear in mind that pruning promotes growth, so where branches have to be lowered or thinned to allow more light, then prune as low as the shrub, tree or conifer will permit. This will encourage branches from the base, leaving them more time to grow before the process has to be repeated.

There are plants, such as rhododendron and yew, that will regrow from stumps. Unfortunately, the poor *leylandii* is not in this category. An alternative conifer would be the Lawson cypress, *Chamaecyparis lawsoniana*. It's not dissimilar in appearance to *leylandii* but it grows at one third the speed and can be maintained annually at two metres.

Dwarf hedges for a garden parterre

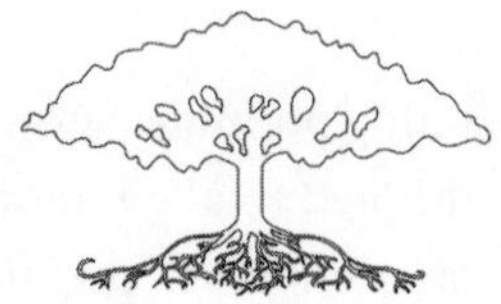

Dwarf hedges have been popular since Elizabethan times, when they were used to form intricate knot gardens. Then the French gave us parterres, complete with edges of low-growing hedge. Today, formal paths edged with evergreen, slow-growing flowering shrubs can still look dramatic – and blend with a modern planting scheme.

It helps if you don't stick to the traditional dwarf box (*Buxus sempervirens* 'Suffruticosa') or lavender (*Lavandula angustifolia*). Box can take an absurd amount of time to clip, it attracts every slug in the neighbourhood and it is also prone to the fungal disease *Cylindrocladium buxicola*, better known as box blight. The unfortunate lavender, on the other hand, is short-lived and intolerant of heavy, wet soil and a damp climate.

I am fond of both, but there are so many other plants that make imaginative alternatives for growing as low hedging.

Site and soil

There are suitable shrubs for sunny or shaded situations. Those with aromatic foliage will do better in full sun and release more of their essential oils. Check there is enough space for the mature plants.

The hedge may not be for life but, with luck, it will be long-term. Thorough preparation of the planting area will help. Dig out perennial weeds such as docks, thistles and nettles, removing all of their roots. Avoid soils contaminated with the really tough weeds such as horse tail, ground elder, coltsfoot and convolvulus.

Where the hedging is to be close-planted it is as easy to dig a continuous trench as to prepare individual planting holes. The trench should be wider and deeper than the plant's root ball. Spread a layer of rotted farmyard manure or compost in the base.

If the roots are tightly packed or congested in the root ball carefully tease them out.

Plant at the same depth as they were in the pot, firming the soil around the roots.

Add a slow-release fertilizer such as bone meal to the topsoil as it is being back-filled at a handful per yard; this will provide steady growth.

Water after planting to make sure air pockets in the soil are eliminated and that it is covering the roots.

Spacing for the plants depends on the variety but for most low-growing shrubs a single row planted 9–18in apart will provide a thick hedge. Regular clipping of foliage hedges in late spring, after all risk of frost is past, will encourage growth and help thicken them at the base.

Plants

Some of the variegated varieties of the evergreen *Euonymus fortunei* make wonderful hedges. *E. f.* 'Emerald Gaiety', which has bright-green leaves margined with white and tinged pink in winter, is compact and bushy.

E. f. 'Emerald 'n' Gold' is similar, with golden variegation replacing the white. Neither are fussy. Both prefer a well-drained soil, sheltered from cold winds and in full sun. They will tolerate light shade but leaf colour will suffer.

Cotoneaster integrifolius is sometimes labelled *C. microphyllus* or *C. thymifolius*. Its small, glossy, evergreen leaves are held on stiff branches. In summer the white flowers open from pink buds followed in autumn by bright-red fruit. As a hedge it needs to be trimmed regularly to prevent it becoming too wide. A short back and sides in late spring and again in autumn will guarantee a dense, attractive hedge.

Gaultheria cuneata deserves to be better known. It forms a tough, hardy evergreen shrub with mid-green leaves. The pure-white flowers appear in late spring and summer followed by small white berries. It will only grow 15in high but, if not clipped in early summer, it will spread to 3ft.

Another *Gaultheria* I really like is *G. mucronata*, which used to be called *Pernettya mucronata*. If the suckers are constantly removed it makes a wonderful compact, dense hedge. The small, glossy dark evergreen leaves are sharply pointed. Urn-shaped white flowers appear in late spring and early summer and are followed in autumn by fruit. To ensure pollination, put in one male plant such as the variety *G. m.* 'Edward Balls', at 3yd intervals. Trim the new extension growths back to the flowering stems in early summer to retain and show off the fruit.

A good substitute for lavender is the aromatic and longer lived evergreen *Prostranthera cuneata*, better known as the Australian or Alpine mint bush. The small, cup-shaped, mid-green leaves exude a strong mint fragrance when crushed and white flowers, each centre marked with purple and yellow, appear in summer. It forms a rounded, compact bush. Clipping the sides annually in late spring will help it keep a straight line. The top can be left unclipped unless it grows higher than 24in.

Staying with aromatic foliage, rosemary is well worth growing as an attractive barrier, and will grow to at least 3 ft in height. The most compact variety is *Rosmarinus officinalis* 'Severn Sea', with evergreen leaves and bright-blue, early-summer flowers on arching branches. It loves a hot, sunny position and well-drained soil. Several of the *Genista* are ideal for a similar situation, especially if the soil is low in nutrients. Although deciduous, they form densely compact bushy plants. *Genista lydia* grows to 24in in height with blue-green leaves and, in early summer, bright-yellow flowers. *G. pilosa* 'Vancover Gold' forms an 18in-high mound of dark-green leaves and golden-yellow flowers in late spring. Dyer's greenwood, *G. tinctoria*, is more upright with dark-green leaves but its variety *G. t.* 'Flore Pleno' produces golden, double flowers in early summer and only grows to 15in high.

Pests and diseases

Fortunately there are no serious pests of these shrubs. An attack of vine weevil grubs at the roots can stunt young plants. The adult beetles will cut notches in the leaves which looks odd but seldom does lasting harm.

Fungus diseases such as *Phytophthora* and *Armillaria* (honey fungus) can do extensive damage and wipe out whole hedges. Isolated portions of the hedge suddenly dying should be examined by an expert and as a precaution dug out and burnt. The soil should be isolated from the remaining plants by an 18in deep barrier of plastic.

Step-overs

For a plant to succeed as a 'step-over' hedge it must have most, if not all, of the following characteristics:

- They should be low, slow-growing, and tolerant of clipping.
- Preferably evergreen – although a dense, twiggy, deciduous shrub such as *Berberis thunbergii* 'Bagatelle' looks good with its deep-red-purple foliage.
- The ability to grow happily when squeezed by the plants on either side.
- Not subject to rampant suckering.
- Resistant to disease.

Summer-flowering trees for any size of garden

Plant one tree and you add height, interest, shape and colour to the garden. Seasonally, trees are acclaimed for their showy spring flowers, their spectacular autumn leaf colour or dramatic winter bark.

Their summer season has, to a large extent, been hijacked by fragrant flowering shrubs, perennials, annuals and the country's favourite, the rose.

The cooling shade offered by a majestic domed chestnut, slimly elegant birch or golden weeping willow is often, in our climate, just a fleeting pleasant memory.

It is the summer-flowering of trees which deserves to be promoted. As spring's crab apple and cherry blossom falls like confetti to top-dress the lawn and avenue, gardeners should make more of the less common summer-flowering trees.

Best trees

No one could possibly dislike *Eucryphias*. They prefer a neutral to acid soil but there are some which tolerate alkaline conditions. The hardiest is *Eucryphia glutinosa*, a beautiful – but not my favourite – upright, deciduous or semi-evergreen tree from Chile with dark-green leaves which turn orange-red in the autumn. Growing to 30ft with a spread of 20ft, it consistently produces fragrant, cup-shaped white flowers in late summer.

Planted in a well-drained, slightly acid soil, an 18–24in high, single-stemmed, container-grown plant will quickly form a flowering tree. Keep the root area cool and well mulched. The head of the tree will benefit from being in full sun.

My personal choice would be *E.* × *intermedia* 'Rostrevor'. It is named after the picture-postcard village in Co. Down squeezed between the Mourne mountains and Carlingford Lough. A mass of large, fragrant white flowers appear in late summer.

For limey soil, grow the evergreen *E.* x *nymansensis* 'Nymansay' with its large white flowers.

Koelreuteria paniculata is often called the 'pride of India' but since it comes from Korea, Taiwan and China I prefer the more descriptive 'golden-rain tree'. The deciduous foliage has a lot going for it with large, pinnate, mid-green leaves which emerge pink then turn to butter-yellow in the autumn.

Large, see-through, pyramidal panicles of small, bright-yellow flowers appear in late summer and are held, in full display, beyond the foliage. There are few other good yellow flowering trees to follow the late-spring laburnum.

Attractive 2in-long, pink, bladder-shaped seed pods follow. It is easily grown by sowing the fresh seed in the autumn and over-wintering the plants under glass. Plant in a fertile, well-drained soil in full sun with sufficient space to allow it to grow to a final height and spread of 30ft. The variety 'September Gold' is later-flowering, with its main show in early October.

Hoheria 'Glory of Amlwch' is evergreen and grows to 20ft. *Hoherias* are from New Zealand but this variety originated in Anglesey. It dislikes cold winds.

Planted in a sheltered site or against a south-facing wall in well-drained, alkaline soil, it will reward you with a blanket of pure-white, fragrant flowers in mid-summer. Glossy, evergreen leaves and a spreading habit extend its seasonal interest.

Oxydendrum arboreum, the sorrel tree, deserves to be better known and more widely planted. Although slow growing, it will produce flowers from an early age.

The glossy, dark-green, deciduous leaves turn to brilliant shades of orange, red and purple in autumn. From July until the leaves colour, large panicles of small, urn-shaped white flowers hang from the tips of the shoots. This tree will grow to 35ft high. It is hardy but prefers to be sheltered from cold winds in a well-drained acid soil. A position in full sun improves the autumn leaf colour.

Stuartia pseudocamellia looks like a camellia and is related but it is deciduous. At 60ft high with a spread of 20ft, it will become too large for many gardens. Where you have space, plant it in a well-drained acid soil with lots of added compost. A sunny but sheltered situation is ideal.

It hates being transplanted so don't think you can get away with moving it when it outgrows a cramped space. The dark-green leaves turn to wonderful autumn shades, while its large, pure-white, cup-shaped flowers with orange-yellow stamens are outstanding during July. Once this tree settles down it will cover itself in flower every summer.

Cladastrus lutea originates in the south-east of the United States, where it is known as 'yellow wood'. It forms a 30ft high deciduous tree, its pale-green leaves turning golden yellow in autumn.

The branches are brittle and easily damaged in an open, windy site. The yellow and white flowers are very fragrant, hanging wisteria-like in long panicles during July. The best flower display follows a long, hot summer when the wood is well ripened, so plant in well-drained soil in full sun.

Growing tips

In sheltered sites small trees may be planted without staking, allowing the tree to build up a strong spreading root system. Larger trees will require a short stake and tree tie to prevent wind rock damaging the roots. Check frequently to ensure the tree tie is not strangling the trunk. Remove the stake when it is no longer required. The hole left through the root ball, when the post is removed, may be filled with a mixture of compost and bone meal.

Other summer-flowering trees

- *Catalpa bignonioides*: large, deciduous leaves. Panicles of white flowers with yellow and purple markings in July and August.
- *Magnolia grandiflora*: large, glossy, evergreen leaves. Pure-white, fragrant flowers up to 10in in size in summer. Needs shelter. Tolerates lime.
- *Magnolia delavayi*: enormous, evergreen leaves. Creamy-white,

fragrant flowers in late summer. Dislikes cold winds. Grows well in alkaline soil.

- *Ligustrum lucidum*: glossy, evergreen leaves. Large panicles of very fragrant white flowers in late summer and early autumn. Dislikes cold winds. Best on an alkaline soil.
- *Liriodendron tulipifera*: deciduous. Tulip-shaped green flowers with an orange band at the base in summer. It does not flower as a young tree. Moist soil in full sun.

Small trees

- *Albizia julibrissin*: needs shelter. Height 20ft.
- *Cornus* 'Porlock': prefers a moist soil. Height 25ft.
- *Eucryphia lucida*: prefers an acid soil. Height 25ft.
- *Hoheria angustifolia*: dislikes cold winds. Height 20ft.
- *Maackii amurensis*: prefers a sheltered site. Height 25ft.

Small trees for a small garden

Small trees are quite at home in any size of garden but if a large growing tree is planted in a small garden then, eventually, both the tree and the garden will suffer.

A suitably sized tree will provide shape and colour, encourage wildlife and add a vertical dimension to the smallest garden.

Many trees are ideal for planting in a large container where they will give pleasure for many years. When the tree becomes too large for the container make a present of it to someone with more space but get the container back for another tree and a further decade of enjoyment.

First on the list is the weeping Kilmarnock willow, *Salix caprea* 'Kilmarnock'. It is deciduous with yellow-brown stems and dark green 4in-long leaves, grey-green on the underside. Silver-grey, male catkins with yellow anthers appear in late spring. It will never grow more than a few inches higher than the top graft where the branches appear. That's usually 5–6ft above ground level on a bare stem. It will succeed in any soil and is tolerant of wet ground. It is usually necessary to keep the tree supported with a timber stake. Remove dead branches inside the canopy to prevent the mature tree becoming widespread.

Another favourite, compact tree is the weeping crab apple, *Malus* 'Royal Beauty'. Its deciduous leaves open red-purple, turning dark green and purple on the underside. The dark-red-purple flowers appear in late spring followed by small, dark-red fruit in autumn, height 6ft with a spread of 8ft.

Choose a site in full sun and well-drained, fertile soil. Every garden should have at least one Japanese maple. *Acer palmatum* 'Chitoseyama' is a slow-growing, deciduous gem with small, deeply lobed crimson-green foliage that turns to a deep-red-purple in early autumn. Plant it in a sheltered site protected from cold winds and late-spring frosts.

Taller but flagpole thin the ornamental cherry, *Prunus* 'Amanogawa', grows to 20ft. Its stiff, upright branches bear mid-green leaves that become yellow, orange and red in autumn. In late spring it clothes itself in dense clusters of pale-pink, fragrant flowers. In maturity it will be broad and may need pruning in summer to retain its slim figure.

Sophora microphylla 'Sun King' forms a bushy tree with a height and spread of 10ft. It is evergreen with pinnate, dark-green leaves and pendant racemes of pea-like, dark-yellow flowers in early spring. It prefers a well-drained site in full sun.

How to move shrubs and trees

October is one of the best months to move plants, trees and shrubs that have either outgrown or no longer suit their allotted space. Plants that are too close to other plants, the path or to buildings – especially if they are obscuring the view – are prime contenders.

Do your transplanting while the soil is still warm with the promise of rain to come. But bear in mind that any plant that's been moved will suffer and it will need plenty of encouragement if it is to re-establish happily.

When large plants need to be transplanted it is best to engage a professional landscape firm. But there's no reason why you shouldn't be able to tackle smaller trees and shrubs with confidence.

Prepare the new site

The first thing you should do is check that the new location is suitable in the long term, since you don't want to have to move the plant again. A few days before the move, dig the planting hole at least 12in larger all round than the root ball. Separate the topsoil and discard the subsoil. Loosen the soil at the bottom and sides of the hole, fill it with water and allow it to drain.

Incorporate a 4in layer of old, well-rotted farmyard manure or compost into the pit base. When planting add a couple of handfuls of bone meal and some compost to the heap of topsoil, then replace it round the roots.

Lifting and replanting

The secret of success is not to let the plant know it has been moved. Water it a few days before digging and lifting it out of the ground, making sure the water has penetrated through the soil to the root.

When you excavate, keep a root ball at least the same diameter as the overhead canopy of branches and leaves. Small plants should have a root ball of 18–24in. Retain as much soil as possible around the roots – if the soil is dry it will crumble and fall off. Tightly wrap the ball of soil in hessian or polythene to hold it in place during the move. Take it in the wheelbarrow or slide it, on a sheet of polythene, to its new position.

Plant at the same depth as before, firming the soil to eliminate any air pockets. Finally, press down with your boot to form a concave dish to retain rain in the area of the roots. Water daily for the first week and regularly afterwards.

If there is a drying wind or a prolonged period of dry weather after planting, spray water over the foliage of evergreens to reduce the amount of moisture transpired through the leaves.

Bare-root and container planting

Trees and shrubs with bare roots are available from November to March, but their success rate after planting depends on their treatment prior to purchase and how well they are planted.

Those in pots can be planted at any time of the year if the soil is in good condition. Avoid planting into cold, wet, sticky soil. When the container is removed any roots visible around the outside of the compost should be white or brown. Blackened roots are probably dead and if there is a significant quantity return the plant to where you bought it.

Make sure the compost is moist before teasing some of the roots out of the root ball, and plant out in the ground at the same depth as in the pot. With bare-rooted plants there will be a soil mark at the base of the stem to show you the planting depth. The planting pit should be larger all round than the root ball. Work the soil through the roots, filling all the spaces as you go. Shake and gently lift the plant to make sure the soil settles evenly. Firm with your foot and dish the surface to retain water. Apply one to two gallons of water immediately after planting and then keep well watered.

Support

Large trees and plants with a poor root system will benefit from a supporting stake until the stem has strengthened and their roots have spread out and taken a firm hold in the ground. To avoid damage, drive the stake into the prepared hole before inserting the plant. Manoeuvre the roots round the post, then tie the trunk with a rubber pad to prevent chafing. Where there is a large root ball the stake can be driven in at an angle from beyond the roots.

How to grow pear trees

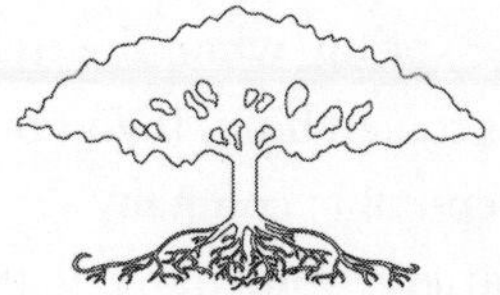

There is nothing more sensuous than biting into a pear so ripe that the juice dribbles down your chin. And when the fruit has been picked from your garden, it is a proud – if undignified – moment.

With attention to detail, it isn't difficult to grow pears. That's not to say that everyone finds it easy, but given suitable soil and reasonable climatic conditions, there are varieties of pear that will perform well in most British gardens.

The key is to choose a sheltered, sunny spot, avoiding low-lying areas where the morning frost lingers. They will suffer badly if exposed to bitterly cold easterly winds, and salt deposits from coastal blasts will cause the foliage to blacken. Pears require more sunlight than apples, so reserve space on a sunny south- or west-facing wall for growing and training at least one pear tree.

Pears demand a fertile, well-drained, moist soil – loam-based is preferable. Avoid waterlogged conditions and heavy clay soils, as these are often wet in winter, then dry out to form a hard, crusty, cracked surface in summer. If planted in chalky soil or on light, sandy ground, they will become stressed, producing poor quality fruit. When planting at the base of a wall, dig a large pit and remove any builders' debris and plaster that accumulated before the topsoil was spread.

Late autumn and early winter is the best time to buy fruit trees. It is worth travelling to a nursery so that you can see what you are buying – and of course spring, when the trees are in full blossom, is a lovely time to start researching. If you buy through mail order, make sure you use a reputable company.

Select a suitable variety from those listed. Check what rootstock the variety has been grafted onto. There will usually be a choice between 'Quince A' and 'Quince C'. The latter will produce a slightly less vigorous plant and is a better rootstock for garden use. When offered for sale as bare-root plants, there should be a strong main framework with a mass of small, thin, fibrous roots. These should be pliable, with no sign of dryness. Roots longer than 12in may be trimmed back. Damaged roots should be cut back to sound material. Cover the roots with damp soil or peat until you are ready to plant. Container-grown trees should have sufficient roots to hold the compost together. Where the roots are congested and form a tight ball, tease out the outer layer before planting; this encourages them to spread out quickly into the soil.

The main stem should be straight, with no damage to the bark. The head of the tree should be well branched without crowding, crossing or rubbing branches.

It is possible to buy two- and three-year-old cordon-, fan-, or espalier-trained pears, where the shape has been established. Only buy trees labelled with the variety and rootstock.

Planting

It really is worth taking time to ensure that the tree is well planted; if happy, a pear tree should produce fruit for twenty years or more. With some rootstocks (except dwarfing), they will fruit regularly for over fifty years.

The planting hole should be at least twice the size of the root area. Separate the topsoil from the hard subsoil, which may be dumped. Fill the hole with water and allow it to seep away. Fork over the bottom of the pit to loosen the subsoil. Place a layer of old, well-rotted farmyard manure in the base of the hole and cover with a layer of topsoil.

Free-standing trees will require a supporting timber stake treated with preservative. Drive the stake into the hole before planting the tree to prevent damage to the roots.

To stop pear trees re-rooting on the stem, they must be planted with the graft union at least 4in above the finished soil level. The graft union is an obvious swelling on the stem close to the base. Spread the roots out and back-fill with topsoil. A few handfuls of bone-meal fertilizer mixed into the soil will get the plant off to a good start.

Firm the soil with your foot as you plant to eliminate air pockets around the roots. Water well after planting and dish the soil surface around the stem to help hold rainwater in the area of the roots. If you have staked the tree, the main stem can be supported and held firm by using a tree tie. A rubber spacer will prevent the stem rubbing against the stake.

Pruning and training

Pears should be pruned in late winter but wall-trained trees such as cordons will require summer pruning as well, to shorten new growth.

For the first few years, pruning is mainly just shaping and training the tree. This creates the framework that will support the leaves, blossom and fruit for the remainder of its life. After this, pruning is used mainly to maintain the tree and generate new fruiting branches.

Bush trees are pruned to build up a multi-branched shape with the stems well spaced to allow as much sunlight as possible to penetrate. The centre of the bush is kept open, with no crossing branches.

For the first two years, strong shoots should be reduced in winter by half their length. Weak stems are cut hard, removing two-thirds of the length. The cut should be made with sharp secateurs or a knife, and slope upwards from a suitable outward-pointing bud. In future years, the side shoots need to be reduced to four or five buds in winter, which will help form a balance of new growth and fruiting branches.

Cordon pear trees are usually trained to grow as a single stem at an oblique angle of 45 degrees. Where possible, they should point north, so they receive as much sunlight as possible.

Where several cordons are being planted, they should be spaced 3ft apart. Tie them along a cane supported on horizontal wires. Use ties of soft twine or raffia, which won't cut into the bark. Allow the main leader to grow to the top of the cane and cut back at this point every spring. Side shoots from the main stem are shortened to three leaves in late spring. Each year they are cut to within 4in of the previous year's cut. Lateral side shoots from the main side shoot are reduced to one leaf each spring.

Espaliers are trained on galvanized wires, with the side shoots extending horizontally on either side of the upright trunk. Space the branches 18in apart. Training is the same as for cordons, but it should be carried out at the end of July, or two weeks earlier in southern counties of England.

Best varieties

- A range of varieties is available, and more than one should be planted to ensure good pollination.
- Self-fertile varieties such as 'Conference' carry more fruit when pollinated with another variety.
- Early-flowering varieties such as 'Louise Bonne de Jersey' can be difficult to pollinate, but produce juicy, sweet fruit with a deep-red flush to the skin in late September.
- Late-flowering pears include 'Concorde', which is great for flavour and produces large, regular crops. It is a pollinating partner for the juicy, red-flushed 'Doyenne du Comice' and for 'Winter Nellis'. The latter is the safest choice for frosty northern gardens.
- 'Conference', 'Beth' and 'Beurre Hardy' are mid-season varieties. 'Conference' produces long, narrow, juicy fruit with firm flesh. It also suits my northern garden, as does the more recently introduced 'Beth', whose skin is pale-yellow when ripe and will crop early in life.

How to grow figs

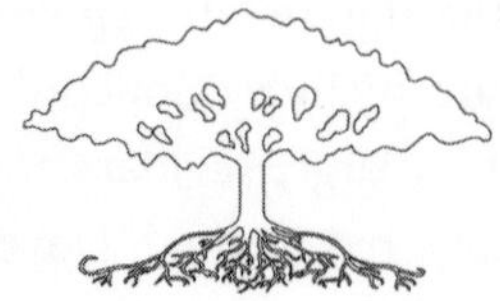

A fresh fig is one of the sweetest and most succulent of fruits. Yet, though the tree is easy to grow, it is hard to get a top-quality crop.

The problem is not so much lack of care, but too much. Gardeners in Britain are the best in the world but we do tend to mollycoddle our plants. This works wonders for most of what we grow but the fig is happy in its misery. It relishes the dry, rocky conditions in its natural home in the Mediterranean. Feed it regularly and it will produce long leafy shoots devoid of fruit.

As plants go, the fruiting fig *Ficus carica*, which is related to the rubber tree, *Ficus elastica*, and the weeping fig, *Ficus benjamina*, is not fussy. Its only demand is for well-drained soil (it cannot tolerate wet, heavy conditions), but a good, well-drained loam will give just as good results as a sandy soil low in humus. Avoid extremes of acidity and alkalinity.

In all but the most favoured sites, figs are best planted and trained against a sunny, sheltered wall. South- or west-facing is ideal. Generally the soil at the base of a wall will be dry and impoverished – exactly the conditions the fig loves. Trained as a fan, the tree will quickly cover an area of wall 15ft across and 10–12ft high. They may be planted any time between October and March, but March is best since the fig is coming into growth. Select a partially trained fan-shaped tree, two to three years old, with a good root ball and healthy shoots and leaves.

Planting

Extra care should be taken when planting. Since figs are not grafted, the planting depth is not critical, but if the roots are not restricted the tree will grow to a large size, making lots of growth at the expense of fruit. To avoid this dig a hole 2ft square and 2ft deep, and line the sides with paving slabs to confine the fig's roots. Use a layer of crushed building bricks in the base to ensure the drainage is good.

Backfill the planting hole with a 50:50 mixture of grit and loam, mixing in 6–8oz of bone meal to act as a slow-release fertilizer. Thoroughly soak the root ball before planting. Make the plant as firm in the soil as possible, then water it copiously to settle the soil around the roots. Figs are not greedy feeders, so a balanced top-dressing of nutrients in the spring is sufficient – but avoid fertilizers with high levels of nitrogen.

Alternatively, your fig could be planted in a container. Choose a pot with a diameter of at least 18in. A half barrel is a good size: any smaller and the fig will be too cramped; larger and it will produce lots of new growth and large leaves.

The container may be sunk into the ground, with its rim slightly above soil level; but if it is placed above ground, on a hard surface, it will need to be watered daily in summer. Use the same planting mixture, leaving at least 3in between the top of the compost and the rim of the container. Again, an annual dressing of new compost may be added in spring. Repotting, when necessary, is best carried out in late winter.

Training the tree as a fan is a continual operation. The stems should be tied at an angle of 45 degrees to the horizontal, on galvanized wires 12in apart and fixed to the wall with eyes. Established trees need to be pruned in June. Cut back newly formed branches, leaving four or five leaves. New fruiting shoots will grow from below the cut: tie these to the wires.

Where the roots are restricted, regular watering is essential in summer and later, when the fruit is swelling. Birds can be real pests, removing pieces from the ripening figs. Covering the tree early on with a fine-mesh net will discourage them – leaving only wasps as a major nuisance.

In late September remove all the remaining small, unripe fruit except for the tiny, pea-sized embryos that form close to the end of the shoots. These will grow away in spring to produce next year's crop.

Figs are not frost-hardy and the ends of the shoots that are carrying next year's crop are susceptible in winter. Drape horticultural fleece over the plant until after the last frost. In spring, cut out any dead branches and remove any new growth that is heading in the wrong direction.

Varieties

- 'Brown Turkey' is the most popular variety for indoor or outdoor cropping in Britain. It is a regular cropper with lots of fruit. The skin is purple-red with sweet red flesh.

- 'Brunswick' ripens earlier than 'Brown Turkey' with good flavour but the crop is light.
- 'White Marseilles' is pear-shaped with white flesh and a good flavour.
- 'Black Ischia' produces small round fruit with purple skin and deep-red, well-flavoured flesh.

Growing tips

Figs are easily propagated. They sucker readily at the base and, since they are grown on their own rootstock, these suckers can be removed already rooted. Layering a low branch in spring by encouraging it to root where it touches the ground will, by the autumn, provide a large plant ready for planting out.

The fruit isn't fertilized and is really the swollen base of the flower. The figs are ready for picking from mid-August, when they bend the stalk downwards. The skin colours and may crack. When a 'fig tear' forms – a drop of nectar at the base of the fruit – it is ripe. Figs are easily damaged by handling.

When there is a glut of fruit, dry the surplus to see you through the winter. Make sure the fruit aren't bruised and lay them individually in a hot press or drying cupboard. Gently turn them each day. They will be dried within a week. On a dreary winter's day, their flavour will bring back summer.

Winter-scented shrubs

For me, this is the best season for fragrance. In summer there is always too much competition from barbecues, suntan lotion and new-mown grass, but the scents of winter-flowering shrubs seem to hang in the cold air, so freely dispensed that there is little need to bury your nose in the flower.

Sarcococca, the Christmas box, is the most wonderful of the evergreen, winter-flowering fragrant shrubs. There are four species; all are hardy and produce tiny, highly scented white or pink-tinged flowers in the dead of winter. These are followed by black, blue-black or deep-red fruit.

The flowers are small enough to go unnoticed among the 2–4in long dark-green leaves. They work overtime producing vast quantities of perfume that will, on a calm day, catch your attention at a distance of 20ft.

There are several *Sarcococca* to choose from. *S. confusa* forms a rounded, bushy shrub 6ft high with a 3ft spread. *S. hookeriana* spreads rapidly by suckers growing 5ft high with a spread of at least 6ft. *S. humilis* has pink-tinged, white flowers and also spreads by suckers but is a more compact plant, growing to 2ft with a spread of 3ft, making it ideal for small gardens. *S. h.* var. *dignya* 'Purple Stem' has pink-tinged flowers and young shoots that are an attractive pale-purple. Less common is *S. ruscifolia*, which has creamy-white, winter flowers and a height and spread of 3ft.

All prefer shade and soil rich in humus that is moist but with good drainage, which makes them ideal for a woodland glade or for planting on the north side of a hedge. A well-rooted sucker of the Christmas box makes a wonderful gardening present.

The incomparable *Hamamelis*, or witch hazel, is a trouble-free hardy shrub that seldom needs to be pruned. They are happy when planted in a sunny or lightly shaded position in an acid to neutral, well-drained soil. Once their oval shaped, green deciduous leaves turn to autumnal shades of buttery-yellow you will be treated to a superb flower show with gorgeous fragrance.

Hamamelis mollis, the Chinese witch hazel, will grow to about 13ft with the same spread. The golden-yellow flowers appear on the bare stems in mid-winter, resembling a cluster of crimped strips of lemon zest. The fragrance is astonishing. From a distance a mature, flowering plant appears as a golden cloud. One of the most desirable varieties is *H. m.* 'Pallida', which has clusters of large, sulphur-yellow flowers in mid- to late winter.

Hamamelis × intermedia has *H. mollis* as one parent and has given rise to many excellent, hardy varieties such as 'Arnold Promise'. It forms a large, open, bushy shrub with good autumn leaf colour and a mass of bright-yellow flowers in winter, which have a pleasant but not far-reaching scent. It is often in flower for Christmas.

Azara integrifolia, an evergreen, isn't fully hardy and requires a sheltered position protected from cold, drying winds. It forms a large, tree-sized shrub with mimosa-like clusters of scented, bright-orange-yellow flower.

You will be well rewarded if you plant *azara* against a south- or west-facing wall. Make sure the soil is moisture retentive and add humus. Lots of old, well-rotted farmyard manure in the base of the planting hole will reap rewards for years to come.

A. microphylla is hardier but of similar habit. It has smaller, bright-green leaves and tiny, vanilla-scented, green-yellow winter flowers, which are formed in the leaf axils on the underside of the leaves. I once spent an hour under a massive bush of *A. microphylla* waiting for the rain to ease. It was February, cold and wet, and the overhead canopy was leaky but the scent was incredible, and looking up into the small flowers was like viewing a starry sky.

Ulex europaeus 'Flore Pleno', the double-flowering gorse, is for you if you enjoy the clean, sweet fragrance of coconut. While this spiky evergreen mainly flowers in spring, it will produce small quantities in winter and throughout the year. Common gorse is as fragrant but it, unlike the double-flowered form, is cursed for setting seed indiscriminately.

Every garden should contain a *Mahonia* and there can be few excuses. They prefer a moist but well-drained soil and are happy in a shaded position. A sunny site is tolerated, providing the soil doesn't dry out.

Mahonia japonica is famous for its glossy, spiky, evergreen and pinnate foliage and is loved for its sweetly fragrant, lemon-yellow flowers that appear in the dead of winter. *Mahonia × media* 'Winter Sun' produces erect racemes of tightly packed, lightly scented bright-yellow flowers which, though more obvious than those of *M. japonica*, have less-noticeable perfume.

I have never grown a *Daphne* that I didn't appreciate. The only complaint I could possibly register is their dislike of transplanting. Most are fragrant in flower and the range of varieties will keep you enthralled from winter until early summer.

I have two favourites for late winter. *Daphne bholua* grows to a large, 8–10ft-high shrub. It retains its leathery, dark-green leaves throughout the year and clusters of fragrant, white, pink-flushed flowers bloom in late winter. The real gem, however, is *D. mezereum*. This forms an upright, deciduous shrub with exquisite flowers that appear in late winter before the grey-green leaves. These pink to purple-pink blooms are highly perfumed and a single sprig will fill a room with scent. It is a tidy plant with a height and spread of 3–4ft, totally hardy and never in need of any pruning.

If you have a warm sheltered wall buy a pot-grown *Lonicera fragrantissima*. In winter, irrespective of weather, this busy, semi-evergreen honeysuckle produces, from the leaf axils, tubular, creamy-white flowers with an incredible fragrance. Plant it at the base of the wall in well-drained soil and water it regularly until it has settled in. In cold, exposed gardens it can turn deciduous. It can be pot-grown and kept in the conservatory during flowering, after which, to restrict growth, prune by shortening all the previous year's growth by two thirds.

Imagine having a whole, winter-scented bed of these shrubs close by the front door. I for one wouldn't mind being left standing on the doorstep.

How to grow holly, ivy and mistletoe

Holly

If you want holly with berries, you must first make sure that you have both male and female plants – otherwise the flowers cannot be fertilized. But with hollies it is easy to be confused. Contrary to what you might expect *Ilex aquifolium* 'Silver Queen' is a male variety while *I.* × *altacierensis* 'Golden King' is female. The sight of a hedge of common English holly, without even a single berry, does not mean that the plants are all male. They could just as easily be a collection of females without a male holly in the vicinity to offer pollen for fertilization.

The only sure method of deciding the sex of an unnamed holly is to examine the plant when it is in flower, usually in late spring or early summer. The flowers are small and white with a hint of green. The male flowers have stamens in which to carry pollen, while in female flowers the stigma is prominently displayed above the ovary.

If you have neither the time nor inclination to go around sexing holly bushes, save yourself the trouble and simply plant a hermaphrodite which has male and female flowers on the same plant. Self-fertile, they include the red berried *I. aquifolium* 'J C van Tol' with dark evergreen, spine-free leaves. Or try *I. a.* 'Pyramidalis', which forms a narrow tree or shrub.

If you're after berries for Christmas you will need to plan ahead and net or bag a few fruiting branches to protect them from the birds.

Which to plant

- *I . a.* 'Mme Briot' is, for once as the name suggests, female with spiny, dark-green leaves brightly edged in gold and bearing brilliant scarlet fruit.
- *I. a.* 'Pyramidalis Fructu Luteo' has mid-green leaves which highlight the mass of yellow berries produced in winter. *I. crenata* 'Ivory Tower' has white berries. *I. crenata* 'Convexa' has black berries.

Growing tips

Holly prefers a deep, moist, free-draining, fertile soil in full sun or partial shade, but it will tolerate most sites that do not get waterlogged.

Ivy

Generally recognized as a vigorous, evergreen climber, ivy scrambles up fences, walls and trees using small, adventitious roots on its stems to hold it to even the smoothest surface. Without support it will swiftly form a thick carpet on the ground, eliminating all but the most persistent weeds.

Hedera helix, the common or English ivy, has many faults but, contrary to belief, it is not a parasite. With my moist, westerly climate it can be a bit of a woody nuisance but it does not live off trees. It has its own root system and simply uses the trees as climbing frames.

Its association with Christmas may stem from its dark, leathery, evergreen leaves which shine when most plants have shed their summer coats.

Once it has reached sunlight the common ivy becomes bushy, producing unlobed leaves on short stems. Clusters of green-yellow flowers appear in autumn, followed by small green berries which turn black. The flowers are a useful source of autumn nectar for bees; blackbirds make short work of the berries.

Which to plant

Garden centres are bulging with ivies, from small-leafed varieties such as *Hedera helix* 'Glacier' with grey and cream variegated leaves to the all green cut-leafed *H. h.* 'Maple Leaf'. 'Congesta' is non-climbing with stiff, upright branches densely crowded with dark-green leaves in opposite pairs. It grows to about 18in in height.

H. h. 'Buttercup' only grows to 6ft high; if it is grown in full sun, the leaves turn an attractive golden-yellow colour.

Growing tips

Ivy will tolerate most conditions but it is happiest in a moist, well-drained, alkaline soil. When ivy is trained to cover a wire mesh support and pruned regularly to build up a solid dense screen it forms a magnificent backdrop to a planted container or figurine.

Mistletoe

Christmas would be less fun without *Viscum album*, better known as mistletoe. Until recently, however, most churches banned it – some still refuse to let it through their doors, as it is traditionally a pagan symbol. Its history precedes Christianity and the plant has had mystical associations for thousands of years.

Like holly and ivy, mistletoe is evergreen, presenting translucent white berries in the dead of winter. It lives without roots by drawing food from other trees, and suddenly appears without invitation.

Mistletoe is easy to grow, though it may not happen at the first attempt. But Christmas is not the ideal time to try propagation, as the branches on sale in markets are often imported from France before the berries are fully ripe. You are more likely to be successful if you can find local berries harvested in February and March.

Growing tips

Make a small incision on the underside of a 4in diameter branch of a suitable tree. Smear the whole berry into the wound in the bark, where its viscid flesh will hold the seed in place. This method of propagation imitates the action of birds as they clean their beaks, removing the seed with it. Bandage the seeded branch with a few layers of damp kitchen roll to prevent other birds from stealing the seed.

Mistletoe is slow to grow, and it will often take a full year before any results are visible. It will then be another few years before you have the means by which to steal a Christmas kiss.

Best plants to climb up trees

Climbing and scrambling plants can make gorgeous companions for trees. Used with imagination, they transform a dull shelter belt into a vibrant extension of the garden, add to the wildlife larder and invigorate a tree that might otherwise appear past it.

Try to choose dedicated climbers that come fully equipped for the job, with no fear of heights. Ideally, once a climber has been introduced to the host tree and given a secure base close to its trunk, it should head for the sunlight. The tree will love the company and the climber will enjoy the freedom to scramble about without running out of support. It will do the host no harm and will help make it more attractive, hiding dead bare branches. And there are other bonuses – including fragrance and flower colour.

Best trees for climbers

Some are better than others but, whatever the species, it is essential the tree is strong and not liable to fall. A vigorous climber will produce a lot of leafy growth that will hold the wind like a sail, putting enormous pressure on the branches, trunk and roots. An old, non-fruiting, cankerous apple tree with lots of branches on a short trunk is an ideal framework.

Conifers are often more in need of camouflage than deciduous trees – pine, spruce and the deciduous larch, for instance, all have bare branches low down.

Imagine a vigorous evergreen *Clematis armandii* climbing through a European larch (*Larix decidua*). In spring, the soft, fresh green tufts of larch leaves will highlight the trailing stems of small white *C. armandii* flowers with their fragrance of almonds. In autumn, as the larch turns to buttery-gold, the long, leathery green leaves of the clematis are waiting to take their place. Similarly, the bright-yellowy tints of *Humulus lupulus* 'Aureus' – hop – look stunning twined round the grey-green foliage of *Picea pungens*, the blue spruce.

Birch, hawthorn and alder are also great hosts, with sufficient branches to allow the climber to run riot. Those growing up trees with more open branches – chestnut, oak, ash or sycamore – need constant training to help them reach the whole framework. In these situations vigorous plants that adhere by aerial roots have a better chance of providing full cover. Good examples are the climbing hydrangea, *Hydrangea petiolaris*, and ivy, *Hedera helix* and its varieties.

Planting

The trouble with underplanting mature trees is their roots: they are always exactly where you want to dig a hole to plant a climber.

Other problems include the state of the soil, which will generally be dry, free-draining and devoid of nutrients; and light levels, which for most of the year will be low under the leaf canopy. With this in mind, plant now and mollycoddle the climber, giving it the conditions to make new growth quickly.

- Site the planting hole as close as possible to the base of the tree and certainly within 2ft.
- Dig as big a hole as possible, avoiding large roots. It should be at least twice the size of the container holding the climber. Smaller roots may be pruned to make space. Remove the soil completely. Fork up the bottom of the hole and add a layer of well-rotted farmyard manure to help conserve water, and add fresh soil from another part of the garden. Pour in three to four gallons of water and allow it to drain. Mix 8oz of bone meal into the new soil and position the root ball in the planting pit.
- With the exception of clematis, keep the plants at the same depth as in their pots. Clematis should be planted with the top of its root ball 4in below the surface to encourage new roots to form on the buried portion of stem.
- Firm the soil round the root ball with your foot, forming a surface dished towards the stem. Water after planting to settle the soil around the roots and eliminate air pockets in the soil. A deep mulch of bark will reduce weeds and help to conserve soil moisture.

Support

Climbing plants haul themselves up into the branches of their hosts using various methods. Some, such as wisteria, twine their stems round the branches. Others, including *Cissus striata*, use tendrils to hold on. Roses use thorns to steady themselves.

A portion of wire netting or plastic trellis can be tied to the bottom of the trunk; hold this out from the bark using small wooden blocks as spacers. This will give the climber something to grip and help the new shoots find their way through the mesh on their way up the tree.

Pruning

One of the secrets of success is in early pruning to encourage the climber to form side shoots. Shortening the main leader will make the plant branch. Each stem can be trained up into a different part of the tree's branch system. Once the climber has taken hold in the tree, there is little need for further pruning.

Fallopia baldschuanica, better known as Russian vine, is too aggressive for arches, pergolas and trellis, but it is ideal in a tree, where it will quickly make 40ft in height. In late summer and autumn the tree will drip, ooze and overflow with panicles of small, pink-tinged white flowers. No pruning is necessary.

With roses it is possible to cut out, at ground level, the oldest stems. They will have to be removed a section at a time to avoid pulling the whole plant out of the tree. Train the rose stems around the trunk, spiralling upwards, and they will produce many more flowering side shoots.

Best climbers for a wall

There is no good reason for having a bare wall in the garden. Walls can be dramatic in a supporting role and a magical backdrop for plants. Yellow winter-flowering jasmine against red brick, red-berried *Pyracantha* trained on white pebble-dash or pink climbing roses over a doorway all have a softening effect. Where there is little or no space, vertical planting is a satisfactory way to garden.

Aspect

North-facing walls tend to be cold and shaded, while south and west are warm and sheltered, making them ideal for fruit and tender plants. East-facing walls get morning sun which, in combination with a frosty spring, destroys early-flowering camellias.

Planting

Improving any existing soil at the base of a wall is usually a must. As you dig down you may encounter a broad band of foundation concrete, forcing you to widen the planting hole. It is likely there will be a thin layer of soil covering the usual builders' debris. Lower down this material forms excellent drainage, but beef up the upper 12–18in with good loamy topsoil enriched with old, rotted farmyard manure.

Close to the wall there is often a strip of dry soil, protected from rain by the roof overhang. Where there is no soil, with a drive or path meeting the wall, form planting holes by cutting through the tiles or tarmac. Alternatively, use containers.

Containers

Choose long-lasting materials such as timber, reconstituted stone or plastic. Avoid earthenware pots that are not guaranteed frost-proof.

The secret of success is to use as large a container as possible, filled with a moisture-retentive, soil-based compost, good drainage holes and plants that can tolerate a restricted root area. Avoid vigorous clematis, such as *Clematis montana*, which prefer to spread their roots far and wide.

Where possible, punch a hole with a crowbar through the hard surface, directly below the container, and fill the mini shaft with soil. Eventually roots will find their way down through the base of the pot and the pot and plant will become a fixture.

Wall plants

There are three groups of plants ideally suited to growing against walls or other verticals. Those that require minimal assistance are self-clinging and include ivy, climbing hydrangea and Virginia creeper. The second group are the scramblers and twiners, such as climbing and rambler roses, clematis, honeysuckle and wisteria. Then there are the free-standing shrubs which, when planted close to a wall, will happily grow up without support. *Garrya, Euonymus, Camellia* and *Pyracantha* are the obvious examples.

Support

With some plants support is essential. Others, such as *Pyracantha*, when trained as espaliers along horizontal wires, form tiers of berried branches. Galvanized or stainless-steel wires are stretched between steel pegs driven into the wall at regular spacings. The pegs have holes drilled through to carry the wire (vine eyes).

Timber, wire mesh or plastic trellis may be fixed to the wall on battens, leaving a 1in gap between wall and support to allow the stems to weave through the trellis.

Training and pruning

Plants that are happiest climbing walls are usually rampant growers with no respect for house eaves, gutters, roof tiles or windows. Annual pruning is needed to prevent damage to downpipes.

Small-leafed ivies such as *Hedera helix* 'Glacier' with its silver-grey, green-and-cream foliage, are less aggressive than the big-leafed variegated *Hedera colchica* 'Dentata Variegata'. *Hydrangea anomala petiolaris* – which has a tracery of bare brown branches in winter and panicles of white summer flowers – and the evergreen *H. seemannii*, with its similar flowers, will glue themselves to any vertical surface, easily climbing to 30ft. They will also tolerate the shade and cold of a north-facing wall.

Parthenocissus tricuspidata 'Lowii', with its deeply cut, brilliant-crimson autumn leaves, often needs to be kept in place for a season until it takes hold.

Twisters and ramblers benefit from training in the early stages to make sure the main stems are directed to cover the whole wall.

There are hundreds of clematis to pick from: the evergreen *C. armandii* has fragrant white flowers in early spring; *C. dioscoreifolia* 'Doctor Ruppel' flowers deep pink in summer; *C. viticella* follows with bell-shaped blue-purple flowers in autumn. They will soon cover any support provided.

For pruning, clematis are divided into three groups. The first are the species, including *C. macropetala*, *C. montana* and *C. armandii*, which are pruned only when they outgrow their space. They can be cut hard immediately after flowering.

The second are the large-flowering clematis varieties that bloom before June, which are pruned in February to remove dead and weak shoots. Cut back to a healthy bud.

The third are the late-flowering hybrids, *C. orientalis* and *C. viticella*, which are pruned in February, removing all the previous year's growth back to the lowest pair of healthy buds.

Without annual pruning and training, the display of flowers on climbing and rambler roses can be disappointing. If the new strong shoots are allowed to grow straight up they will mainly flower at the top. When arched over and tied into place they throw short side shoots, all of which carry flower. In winter, cut out the old stems as close to the base as possible and train in the replacement shoots produced during the summer.

Wisteria can be more unruly than beautiful, with rampant growth and few flowers. The secret to success is to prune twice, cutting the side shoots back to five leaves in summer. In winter, again shorten these shoots to two to three leaf buds. This ripened wood will flower the following year.

Pyracantha does not need support but if its evergreen branches are trained along wires the red, orange or yellow berries will make a great winter show.

Tree fruit such as apple, pear, cherry and fig crop well when grown against a sunny south- or west-facing wall. Trained to horizontal wires and pruned to reduce the side shoots they are of interest all year with flower in spring, fruit in autumn and the cordon, fan or espalier shape outlined in winter.

Early flowering camellias such as 'Donation' dislike morning sun so avoid walls facing east. *Ceanothus arboreus* 'Concha' is an evergreen with deep-blue flowers in late spring. *Garrya elliptica* 'James Roof' produces its 8in-long, silver-grey, male catkins in winter.

Plants to hide bare rose stems

There are few more pleasant sights than summer roses, but, like so many plants, they are seasonal, and from November until mid-June they have nothing to offer. There are, however, ways to disguise this.

To improve their winter appearance, try reshaping rose beds that have been cut out of the lawn. A sweeping curve looks much better than an area bordered by straight lines. A surface mulch of brown compost, old, well-rotted manure or composted bark will contrast with the green lawn. Pruning in early winter to shorten long stems will also make the bed look more presentable.

Try to select plants that will hide the bare soil and make a show while the roses are hibernating. They should be mat-forming to reduce weeds, and low-growing so they don't make pruning difficult.

Flowers, berries or foliage are also useful when the roses are out of flower. Add a preference for evergreen plants and you have the perfect companion for the rose.

The hardy, tuberous *Cyclamen hederifolium* and *C. coum* will make attractive winter cover. *C. hederifolium* has tiny, scented, pink flowers in late autumn, in advance of the patterned leaves. *C. coum* performs well in winter and early spring. In both cases, the carpeting leaves will form a solid layer no higher than 4in high. *Alchemilla mollis* is worth growing beneath roses from spring onwards: it will happily ramble upwards into the stems of the flowers; combine with campanulas for a cottage-garden feel.

Avoid leafy bulbs such as daffodils and tulips. The roses will be coming into flower by the time their leaves are sufficiently yellow to be raked off the bed. Tying them in knots or using a rubber band to bend the clumps of leaves only highlights the mistake.

Most people know *Gaultheria procumbens* as checkerberry. When crushed, its glossy, dark evergreen leaves exude the fragrance of wintergreen. Small, white or pink urn-shaped flowers appear in summer, followed by aromatic, scarlet berries that will persist until spring. While it only grows to 6in in height, it will spread quickly to cover the gaps between rose plants. *Gaultheria myrsinoides* has a similar habit of growth, with tiny, dark, evergreen leaves. If left by the birds, its deep-purple berries will last all winter.

The bugle plant, *Ajuga reptans* 'Multicolor', forms a carpet of bronze-green leaves splashed with pink, red and cream. The dark-blue flowers appear during late spring and early summer.

Thyme makes an excellent aromatic carpet. It is at its best when the roses are in flower, but the mat of tiny, evergreen leaves is attractive all year. *Thymus richardii* grows to 4in, producing purple flowers in late spring. *T. leucotrichus* forms a compact plant with grey-green leaves and pale-pink flowers in spring.

Planting tips

- Plants should be spaced so that they will eventually cover the bed without smothering one another. To avoid damaging the rose roots, plant them between, rather than beside them. If they are planted too close to the perimeter of the bed they will spoil the edge and smother the grass verge.
- Seasonal planting using winter-flowering pansies and polyanthus can look contrived and take up a lot of time planting and lifting. If they are not regularly dead-headed, seed pods form which reduce further flowering.
- Carpeting the rose bed with evergreens will succeed only if any perennial weed roots have been eliminated. Weeding through a rose bed isn't easy, but when the ground is covered with wiry stems and foliage it becomes impossible.

Plants for ponds

A well is for water, a pool is for swimming and – I've always thought – a pond is for plants. But the sad truth is, lots of ponds have neither plants nor drinkable water. They need aquatic varieties to create interest, enhance the appearance and improve the quality of the water.

Such plants go a long way towards maintaining a balance in the pond and reducing the levels of algae that can turn the water into something like pea soup. They are of enormous benefit to wildlife, not only offering protection from predators but also providing food and a safe exit.

There are three groups of plants to consider, and ideally you want a mixture of all of them for a well-balanced water feature.

1. Container-grown

These spend their lives in containers in the water, sending their leaves and flowers up to the surface. This group includes the beautiful flowering waterlilies with their large floating leaves. There are lily varieties to suit water depths from 6in to 36in. *Nymphaea* 'Froebelii' has deep-red, star-shaped flowers and is ideal for water 6in to 12in deep. At the other end of the scale, *Nymphaea alba*, the common waterlily, with its 12in leaves and creamy-white flowers, can handle depths of 3ft.

Stand the plant in its container on an upturned pot with its leaves on the surface. As the leaf stem grows the plant may be lowered until it sits on the bottom and the leaves are starting to spread. These plants prefer a sunny sheltered position and dislike moving water, so place them well away from cascades, waterfalls or droplets from a fountain.

Water hawthorn, *Aponogeton distachyos*, has leathery leaves and produces fragrant white flowers during summer from depths of up to 24in.

Large leaves on the surface provide shade and reduce the spread of algae, which depend on sunlight for growth.

2. *Marginal plants*

These are happy to paddle their feet in shallow water along a ledge but would drown if it went over their heads. They soften the edge of a tiled surround and camouflage the exposed side of the pool.

There are plenty to choose from, including *Houttuynia cordata* 'Chameleon' with its red stems and leaves splashed with red and yellow. It will grow 12in to 18in high and can tolerate 2in to 3in of water. I love the double buttercup-yellow flowers of the marsh marigold, *Caltha palustris* 'Flore Pleno'.

For the larger pond try *Lysichiton americanus*, commonly called the yellow skunk cabbage. The bright-yellow spathe appears in late spring followed by large, mid-green leaves. It will grow to 4ft in height sitting in 1in to 2in of still or moving water. The musky smell is unpleasant but only noticeable when there is a large colony in flower.

3. Submerged plants

This group, commonly called pond weed and also known as submerged or oxygenating plants, plays a vital role in the ecosystem. Their feathery leaves release oxygen, manufactured as a by-product of photosynthesis, directly into the water. The oxygen helps to sustain other life forms. These plants are often dumped into the water and left to fend for themselves, which they do remarkably well, quickly spreading over the available area. They will be easier to manage if small bundles are planted in containers of aquatic compost lined with hessian and top-dressed with gravel to prevent the compost clouding the water.

Once established they spread quickly and need to be thinned regularly to prevent them dominating the pond. No doubt friends and neighbours will be happy to dump a load of their thinnings at your front door. Personally I would put them on the compost heap. They are probably laced with minute pieces of duckweed. Too small to wash off, they will quickly multiply in your pond.

Lagarosiphon major is semi-evergreen and forms a mass of fragile stems covered in scale-like olive-green leaves. It can grow in water 3ft deep. *Hottonia palustris* (water violet), with light-green foliage, produces pale-pink flower spikes held above the water. It is a fast grower and tolerates water to a depth of 18in.

Quantities

The number of plants required obviously depends on the size of the pond. With marginal plants in containers, the only limit is the amount of space available.

A small 8ft by 6ft pond will need 12 bundles of oxygenating plants and one waterlily. For a larger pond in the region of 20ft by 12ft you will need 60 bundles of oxygenating plants and five to six waterlilies. In the same way that an oasis surrounds desert water your pond will blend into the surrounding garden if there are suitable companion plants.

Bog gardens

Establishing a bog garden near the pond extends the range of plants that can be associated with water. It is a useful catchment area for the overflow from the pond. Incorporating moisture-retentive peat, leaf mould and old compost will ensure the ground doesn't dry out in summer. Moisture-loving plants should be placed as close as possible to the edge of the water so you can enjoy their reflections. *Hostas*, with their big leaves variously marked and variegated, are an obvious choice. Candelabra primulas such as *Primula bulleyana* (deep orange), *Iris sibirica* (blue), *Lobelia* 'Cherry Ripe' (scarlet), *Astilbe* 'Venus' (pink) and the giant cowslip, *Primula florindae* (fragrant sulphur yellow), are all easily grown and propagated by self-sown seed and the division of large clumps.

Bigger shrubs, including the dogwoods (*Cornus*) with their bright red or yellow stems, are conspicuous in winter. Large-leafed perennials such as *Rheum palmatum* 'Atrosanguineum', the ornamental rhubarb with its 6ft-high red flower spikes, and *Rodgersia podophylla* with its bronze-green, chestnut-like leaves, are spectacular but fade in comparison to those of *Gunnera manicata* whose leaves grow to 6ft.

Care needs to be exercised when including trees in the design. Leaves must be kept out of the water and, while a covering net in autumn often solves the problem, it is sensible to plant small-leafed species. *Betula pendula* 'Youngii' is a graceful weeping birch with leaves that colour to butter yellow in autumn.

Japanese maples enjoy dappled shade but need to be sheltered from cold winds in spring. *Acer palmatum* 'Garnet' has small, deeply dissected, bright-red leaves. Positioned with precision and overhanging a still pond, with a bright-blue sky reflected on the water, 'Garnet' is a memorable summer sight.

Water care

If you want crystal-clear water try floating plants and waterlilies to shade at least half the pond surface.

- Use submerged plants to add oxygen.
- A fountain or waterfall will raise oxygen levels.
- Remove leaves and organic matter before they decompose.
- Don't use nitrates or ammonia-based fertilizer.
- Encourage wildlife.
- Use rainwater to top up.

Container gardens for balconies

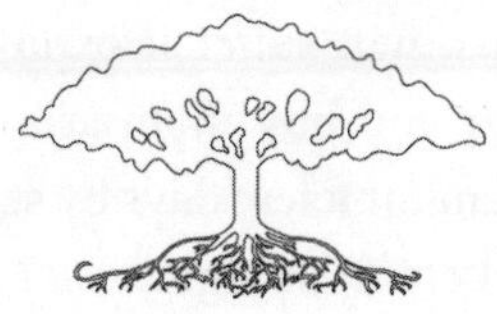

Even in autumn and winter it is often mild enough to sit outside, and that's when you really get the benefit of a well-planted balcony or patio in a sheltered spot. And even when it's cold, looking out of the window at cheerful, colourful plants lifts the spirits.

If you're planting a balcony for the first time, check that it is load-bearing. Containers and their compost can be heavy. Plastic pots and soil-less compost weigh less. If you are planting a patio, use a soil-based medium because it will need less watering in summer.

A balcony or patio that faces south or west will be more sheltered than one exposed to northerly or easterly winds. Strong, cold winds can be detrimental to many plants and it may be worth erecting a wind break using woven willow panels or a temporary sheet of fine plastic mesh. Glass panels can be attached to balcony railings, allowing maximum light to the plants while cutting the blast.

Grow a few permanent plants – most of your planting will be temporary – in large containers to provide an air of maturity. Aim for a year-round effect; evergreens should top the list. Plants that perform for only a short season should be paired up with others that flourish at a different time of year, so that one partner takes over the show from the other.

Your plants should be hardy, with flowers and foliage tolerant of cold, rain and wind. Winter-flowering bedding plants, such as pansies and polyanthus, will suffer if exposed to freezing conditions immediately after you buy them at a warm, indoor garden centre. Acclimatize them for a few days by setting them out during the day and bringing them in at night.

Climbers

Clematis cirrhosa var. *balearica* flowers continuously in winter. Its ferny foliage turns an attractive bronze, making a good backdrop for its pale-yellow flowers spotted with reddish-purple. *Clematis cirrhosa* 'Wisley Cream' has large, creamy-white flowers. Allow it to scramble through *Mahonia* × *media* 'Winter Sun', a shrub with glossy, spiny leaves and fragrant racemes of yellow flowers early in winter.

Lonicera fragrantissima flowers best when planted against a wall. It forms a semi-evergreen shrub with small, fragrant, creamy-white flowers in winter and early spring. When grown in a container, it benefits from hard pruning after flowering. With mature plants, remove a third of the oldest branches at soil level in late spring.

Early bulbs

Bulbs such as snowdrops, *Iris reticulata*, *Cyclamen coum* and crocus come into their own as temporary features. As soon as they finish flowering, remove and replace with another plant in flower.

Heathers

Winter-flowering heathers, *Erica carnea*, love the wind in their hair and the rain on their cheek. 'King George' produces deep-pink flowers in early winter; then comes 'December Red'. 'Springwood White' and 'Springwood Pink' are mat-forming varieties that flower from mid-winter until late spring. Varieties of *Erica* × *darleyensis* are bushy shrubs growing to 12in.

Dwarf conifers

A few dwarf conifers are good companions for heathers. When selecting plants, don't be fooled by labels that say the plants are slow-growing: there is a difference between a dwarf and a slow-growing plant. *Juniperus communis* 'Compressa' is a slow-growing dwarf eventually forming a tight, spindle shape of bright-green foliage 30in high. *Thuja occidentalis* 'Rheingold' forms a conical bush 6ft tall, with golden-yellow foliage, pink-tinged when young. *T. o.* 'Golden Globe' slowly forms a golden yellow sphere 3ft tall.

Dwarf shrubs

Try planting *Skimmia japonica* in the same container as *Jasminum nudiflorum*. The colour combination is a delight.

Hebe ochracea 'James Stirling' has bright, old-gold foliage that gleams like polished brass in rain.

Berries

Whether coated in frost, glistening in the rain or bowed under a coat of snow, berries brighten a dull day. The smell of the crushed leaves of *Gaultheria procumbens* gives it its common name of wintergreen. Clusters of aromatic, scarlet berries persist on plants that only grow to 6in in height.

Skimmia japonica subsp. *reevesiana* forms a compact, evergreen mound with deep-red berries. Mini-standards, 24in high, of red-berried *Cotoneaster conspicuus* add height and interest to containers of dwarf bulbs.

Fragrance

Christmas box, *Sarcococca confusa*, is an evergreen with tiny, creamy-white flowers in winter, followed by shiny black berries. Its perfume is incredibly sweet. For the tail end of winter, plant *Daphne mezereum*. Its scented, purple-red flowers appear on bare stems. Underplant with an ivy such as *Hedera helix* 'Goldchild'.

Wild about saffron

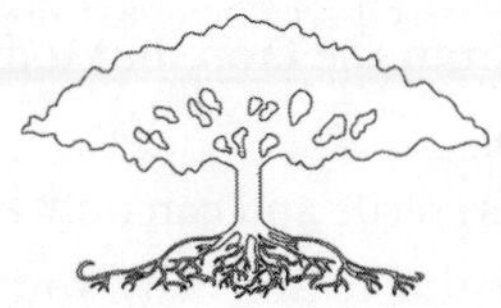

When the English East India Company imported spices in the eighteenth century they attracted high prices and were only affordable to the rich. Now most of them can be bought for next to nothing from every supermarket and corner shop.

Saffron is one of the exceptions. By weight it is more expensive than gold – and you won't find it in the special offers bin. When you look into the wide lilac flowers of *Crocus sativus* it is difficult to credit that the three thread-like, deep-red stigmas are the saffron used in colouring food and medicinally. They are joined at the base to become the style, the reproductive part of the flower.

Crocus sativus is mainly cultivated in countries bordering the Mediterranean that enjoy hot, dry summers. Grown from a corm, in autumn it produces between one and five fragrant, deep-lilac flowers with purple veins. The long, three-branched style, held beyond the bright-yellow stamens, is conspicuous in the centre of the flower. Mid-green, 3in-long leaves with a white, longitudinal line on the upper surface appear at the same time or shortly after the flowers.

Its origin is barely known: the name crocus is derived from the Greek *kroko*, meaning thread; it is part of ancient Greek myth and saffron is mentioned in the Song of Solomon. Experts believe it may be an ancient Greek selection of *C. cartwrightianus* native to Crete. Saffron Walden in Essex was an important centre of cultivation, taking its name from the crop, but today it is mainly grown in south-eastern Spain.

The saffron crocus is sterile and can only be reproduced by division. However, there is no reason why you can't grow your own supply of genuine saffron, as good as that you can buy and all for the price of the crocus corms.

Site and soil

In cold or exposed sites *C. sativus* is reluctant to flower; it prefers a warm, sunny situation in a free-draining alkaline soil. Avoid shaded areas and heavy, clay soils. The corms are dormant in summer and do best in a dry, sandy soil.

Crocus may be naturalized in grass but it is easier to harvest the stigmas if the corms have been planted in rows in a raised bed.

Growing in pots

Planting in containers and window boxes is ideal for those with small gardens or unsuitable soil. The containers can be moved to give the crocus the conditions it likes: hot and sunny in summer, cooler in the autumn to encourage flowers. Use a soil-based compost with added grit for drainage and organic matter in the form of old, well-rotted farmyard manure. In early summer the foliage turns yellow and dies and the corms may be lifted, dried off and stored until replanting in August.

The corms are planted deeper than is usual for other ornamental crocus – 5–6in deep is about right. Space the corms 6in apart. Leaf mould or well-rotted farmyard manure can be incorporated into the soil before planting, adding lime if necessary.

Traditionally August is the planting time but where corms have been dried off or delivered early I believe they will suffer less and are better in the ground from as early as June. If possible buy bigger corms as they will produce more flowers. Each mature corm is capable of providing up to ten flowers over a two- to three-week period.

Growing outdoors

Plant the corms firmly on loose soil with the pointed end up. Remove stones or lumps of soil before back-filling over the corm. Mark the planted area in case something else is planted on top.

In cooler climates flowers appear in early October before the leaves. During warm autumns it starts to flower in mid-September with the leaves competing with the flowers.

Harvesting

There are two methods of harvesting. The stigmas can be nipped off the flowers in situ removing as much of the style as possible. The purple flowers with their yellow stamens will continue to provide colour in the garden. Alternatively the whole flower can be removed before it opens and the red threads can be harvested indoors.

Saffron is expensive because so many flowers are needed to produce even a small quantity. Or, to put it another way, 500 flowers providing three strands – 1,500 strands – will give three grams of dried saffron. The stigmas of 70,000 crocus flowers will, when dried, make approximately 1lb in weight of saffron. No wonder it's valuable.

Dried saffron can be stored and has a superior flavour. If left for a few days on absorbent paper in the airing cupboard it will lose some of its colour but the flavour will improve.

Propagation

Corms multiply quickly and should be lifted and divided when the foliage has died down. If this is done every third year it will avoid overcrowding and loss of flowers. The small corms can be planted separately until they fill out and flower.

Feed the foliage after the saffron has been harvested; using a liquid feed of tomato fertilizer will help the corms to swell.

An area of two square yards will hold 100 corms. Once established and cropping well each corm will produce a minimum of five flowers per year. It doesn't sound a lot but it goes a long way – and it's free.

Pests and diseases

Slugs and snails can create havoc with the emerging flowers. Traps baited with milk or beer are effective providing the bodies are removed daily. Mice, voles and squirrels have a habit of finding the corms and all you can do to prevent them is place fine netting on the soil surface. Birds occasionally strip the flowers. Examine the corms regularly in storage. Any that show signs of rot should be removed and dumped.

PART III
Cushnie Design

Designing a small garden

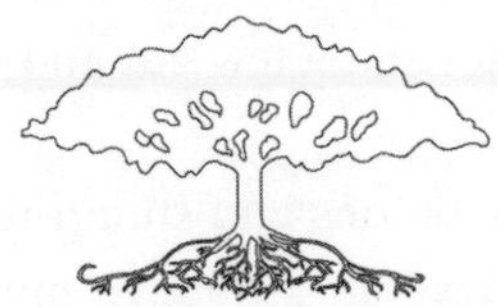

Designing and landscaping a small garden can be a challenge. Using plants that won't become enormous while managing to make the garden look large is tricky. But the real imponderable is how to satisfy a client who aspires to great things – and many of them.

It is not unusual to be handed a list of features that would fit into a football pitch – just. But let's not blame the clients. They may have downsized or are the proud owners of their first garden. Whatever their circumstances, it is the designer's job to do everything possible to implement their wish-list.

What I am frequently asked to do, but refuse to contemplate, is a show garden where the client wants a mature garden overnight packed full of plants that need space.I have no idea why it should be difficult to understand that a show garden is for a week and is then dismantled – whereas the client's patch is ongoing and, we hope, better each year. Size may matter, but small is beautiful. But achieving the impossible isn't as difficult as keeping within a credit-crunch budget, so here is some food for thought.

Edible edges

Speaking of food, it is possible to grow fruit and vegetables in the smallest of gardens. Plant a few alpine strawberries around the side of a hanging basket and a few cut-and-come-again lettuce in the compost on top.

Sow a line of spring onions and stump-rooted carrots between the lettuce and you have an attractive mini-vegetable and fruit garden that is immune to slugs, snails and the low-flying carrot fly.

Think in layers

If your wish-list includes gems such as a rockery, pond and patio, then you can double up or even go for a triple-decker in the same area. Dig a hole 3ft x 19in x 1ft deep. Use a liner with a 20-year guarantee. The excavated soil can be mounded beside the pond and turned into a small rockery and scree bed using a few rocks and gravel.

Plant alpines into pockets of weed-free topsoil. Lift the water from the pond up to the top of the rockery by submersible pump and allow it to trickle back down through pieces of rock laid on a strip of liner.

Electricity should be from a waterproof exterior plug. Surround the rockery and pond with a patio sufficiently large for a table and a few deck chairs. The whole area may be as small as 10 sq/yd.

Under cover

Another combination that gains Brownie points in a small space is a timber pergola over the patio. Use timber trellis panels to enclose three sides and plant with dwarf apple, pear and fig trees. Train them as espaliers.

You now have a sheltered, private sitting area with spring blossom and fresh fruit. Training a vine such as 'Boskoop Glory' over the timber rafters will allow you to swing from your hammock supported on the pergola uprights while you peel your grapes!

Tips for small spaces

- Edge paths with herbs such as thyme, lavender and prostrate rosemary. These give off a wonderful aroma as you brush against the foliage and you'll keep the kitchen supplied.
- Try to provide colour all year. It can be flower, leaf, berry or bark, but make sure that there is something interesting in winter when weather forces us to look out rather than be out.
- Use vertical surfaces and walls to support climbers and shrubs that add height and interest without sacrificing space.
- Fellow designers: always give thanks when the 'must have' list is sensible and a croquet lawn, hot tub and wild flower meadow have been omitted.

How to create a Japanese garden

The Japanese garden is usually described as tranquil, peaceful and an area for contemplation. For me this is understandable. It is the one place in the garden where I can relax and gaze around without the constant reminder of jobs that demand immediate attention.

Position and preparation

The area need not be large but, where possible, it should be as far as possible from the bustle and noise of children's play, and the irritating sound of grass being cut. The site can be in full sun or shade; sun with some dappled shade is ideal. An irregularly shaped plot of ground can be interesting, but try to avoid sloping ground.

Use a glyphosate-based chemical weedkiller to treat perennial weeds before construction; alternatively, they can be dug out by the root, making sure that no pieces are left in the ground to re-grow. While preparing the site, consider a place for a mature tree in keeping with the overall size of the garden: this will give a feeling of permanence. Keep your design simple while allowing your imagination to run riot.

Rocks and stonework

Lay a sheet of landscape fabric to reduce the risk of weeds, and surface the whole area in sand. Several different grades and colours of sand may be incorporated.

A few large, weathered rocks will be the main attraction. They can be bought from most garden centres, and you should choose large stones and ask for them to be delivered. The rocks could be basalt, limestone or granite, and should be similar in texture and appearance. If you like moss, it will quickly colonize the surface of weathered granite. Large rocks dotted through the landscape should be secured in a concealed bed of concrete.

A river or stream can be represented symbolically by a line of round, river-washed pebbles, positioned to form a slow-moving, meandering 'stream'. Flat rocks securely bedded in mortar could be used as 'stepping stones'.

A gently flowing river is a wonderful addition to any garden feature. The sound and sight of water in a Japanese garden are almost hypnotic. But constructing a hidden reservoir and a submersible pump to transport the water through the landscape is a job for another day.

Garden centres and DIY stores stock a range of pseudo-Asian stonework, including figures, lanterns and shrines. Take care with your selection as many are garish and will stand out like weeds in a conservatory.

Boundaries

Perimeter screens of woven bamboo and panels of split canes will offer shelter, screening and privacy to the Japanese garden.

Rocks, stonework and sand

The sand surface needs to be at least 4in deep to allow you to rake patterns into it. Make a few wooden rakes with various sizes of 'teeth'. Set aside some time every day to rake patterns into the sand – it is the most therapeutic gardening job imaginable. A one-ton bag of sand will cover approximately 10 sq/yds at a depth of 3–4in. Mounding the soil before laying the sand will allow you to form contours and a bed for the 'stream' of stones.

Planting

There is no need for extensive planting. A few specimen plants with interesting shapes and colourful foliage are all that is required.

- Clumps of bamboo look natural in a Japanese garden. Most garden centres will have a selection of species and varieties, with canes maturing to black, green, yellow or striped. The slightest breeze passing through a leafy clump causes the foliage to rustle and sigh.
- A Japanese cherry such as the upright *Prunus* 'Amanogawa', with its fragrant, pale-pink, late-spring flowers and superb autumn leaf colour will add height and interest to the garden.
- The dwarf mountain pine, *Pinus mugo* 'Gnom' will, when planted close to a large rock, give the impression of an established landscape.

- Where space allows, plant a magnolia. *M. stellata* produces star-like, pure-white flowers in early spring, before the leaves.
- For character and shape, include the corkscrew hazel (*Corylus avellana* 'Contorta').
- A single specimen of *Acer palmatum* 'Chitoseyama', with its deeply lobed leaves, crimson and green in summer turning to rich purple red in autumn, will complete the planting.

Finishing touches

Use outdoor lighting to pick out individual plants and rocks. Even in the dead of winter, the moving shadows of bamboo will keep the garden interesting. A stone bench may be more authentic, but one made of timber will be more comfortable for those relaxing moments in your new Japanese-themed sanctuary.

The family garden

If you have a family home, your garden should be a family garden. In a garden that will be used by young children, there may have to be 'no-go' areas, but most of it should be fit for playing in without too many restrictions.

Site

Setting aside a dedicated area for play prevents conflicts of interest. It doesn't have to be large but, if young children use it, it must be visible from the house, patio or sitting area. Don't site it under large trees: they can be dangerous. Fence the play area, for safety, and make sure the gate is secured on the outside, beyond the reach of little hands.

Surface

Grazed knees and sore bottoms are part of growing up, but it's still a good idea to provide a soft landing. Use sand or medium-grade bark mulch. Lay the mulch on top of landscape fabric to keep weeds down.

These materials have one drawback: if there are dogs or cats in the garden, they will use this area as a lavatory. A fence will keep dogs out, but is no barrier for a cat. An alternative is coir matting, which can be laid below play equipment when needed, and taken up and stored when it is not.

Try to eliminate grass. Not only does it stay wet after rain, but it also needs constant cutting, and every toy has to be picked up before you can start to mow. Gravel paths remain dry underfoot, and ¼in grade won't shift much during play.

Growing pleasures

Children are never too young to enjoy growing plants. Mark out an area close to, but outside, the playground, and fence it to prevent trampling of the seedlings.

A simple timber fence – such as a 'ranch-style' fence, made from two or three 6in boards, spaced 6in apart – will look attractive. A paving-slab path down the middle will keep boots free of mud after rain.

Keep the growing area small, in a sunny position and free of perennial weeds. Dig the patch, adding compost or rotted farmyard manure, and remove debris and large stones before handing it over. Children love quick results. Help them choose plants that are quick to mature. Feed a weak liquid fertilizer once a week to speed up growth. A trowel, fork and their own gloves will enable them to work the soil.

Design your garden to look big

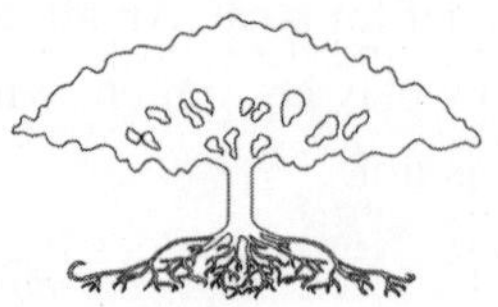

A modestly sized garden can be beautiful, especially if it is treated in a sympathetic manner. It can also be made to look and feel larger. When viewed from the house, any object that draws your eyes to the furthest end will give the impression of a greater space.

Planting a suitably sized tree such as a *Prunus* 'Amanogawa' in the far corner will, when it is in flower or with autumn leaf colour, attract attention. For a dramatic display of shadows light up its bare, upright, winter branches. If all the interesting plants are outside the window or at the door then that is what will be remembered and your garden will shrink rather than expand.

Planning

The first step is to familiarize yourself with your plot. Measure it up and get to know its attributes and problems. Is the soil heavy and wet and in need of drainage? Is it drenched in sunlight or on the cold, shaded north side of the house? Select plants which enjoy the conditions that you can offer.

Be inventive

It is amazing how many plants you can sensibly plant in a small garden. In the space reserved for a bulky pampas grass you could construct a miniature scene from the Alps complete with a wheelbarrow full of tiny alpine gems.

Think positive and be prepared to create illusions of grandeur. It should be possible to accommodate more than one 'outdoor room' in all but the smallest of gardens.

The patio area will double as a secret garden and when sited under a timber pergola the sides and roof can be draped with climbing and trailing plants.

Boundaries

The boundary fence should be planted with shrubs and climbers to provide an interesting vertical dimension. Wall- or fence-trained fruiting plants such as apple, pear and loganberry will provide food as well as shape, texture and height. Where there is a perimeter field hedge keep it low and within bounds. Interplant with honeysuckle, spindle, hazel, holly and shrub roses. That way it will look good all year and provide a great habitat for wildlife.

Where there is a token, low wire-mesh fence between adjacent properties share a mixed shrub and perennial bed with your neighbour.

If you each plant a narrow strip of ground you will enjoy your neighbours' plants and they yours. This way the border will have double the display without encroaching too far into either garden.

Paths

A path should lead somewhere rather than come to a dead end, leaving visitors with no option but to retrace their steps. Design it to meander through all parts of the garden.

An inviting seat at some point will suggest that it is time for a rest and visitors will go away remembering that they took a break when walking around your garden. Wherever possible form short side paths, their length camouflaged with suitably positioned evergreen plants. Use stepping stones in preference to a continuous path to cross a small lawn or to cut through a bed of shrubs.

Gravel paths can be planted on either side with mat-forming plants such as thyme, that will soften the edges and creep over the surface. Paths that are edged with low-growing hedges of box or lavender have a narrow appearance.

Planting

Be consoled that gardeners never have enough space for plants and for that reason impulse purchase of desirable shrubs and perennials is to be discouraged. Always have a spot in the garden in mind before you trek off to the garden centre and always be sure to check the ultimate size and spread of every plant.

The good news is that you will be able to grow several layers of plants. Ground-covering shrubs that tolerate shade, such as *Pachysandra terminalis* and the periwinkles (*vinca*), may be planted under other shrubs and where there is shade cast by tall trees, another tier of medium-height shrubs such as camellias can be incorporated.

Spring bulbs such as wood anemone and snowdrop will flower and die down long before the bulk of garden plants are making a display.

Patios and seating areas

Don't forget to include a patio. I have seldom seen a garden too small for a sitting area. It doesn't have to be a landing pad for helicopters. Retain all the hard surface area for seats and a table. Don't clutter it with lots of containers. Rely on plants close by to provide colour and fragrance. Where the patio is beside the dwelling then you can attach mangers to the wall and fill them with seasonal bulbs, fragrant plants, trailing annuals, herbs or strawberries.

The barbecue should be portable, only taking up space when it is in use. On a small patio a double swing lounger is probably a luxury you will have to sacrifice. Settle for a tubular-framed hammock instead.

If you want to make compost then go out and buy a compost bin. The amount of space it will occupy is more than compensated for by the end product. It can be tucked behind an evergreen shrub, accessible but camouflaged.

Choose plants that look good for long periods. Evergreen shrubs will provide leaf shape and colour when not in flower.

Amelanchier 'Ballerina' is a medium-sized, deciduous tree that can be kept to a reasonable size by pruning. The emerging leaves are bronze, turning to mid-green and taking on brilliant autumn shades of red and purple. The small, white, spring flowers are followed by sweet, juicy fruit that ripen from red to purple-black. Avoid perennials that are rampant.

You can have too much of a good thing and a bijou garden plastered with *Alchemilla mollis* (lady's mantle) will soon become boring.

Annuals may be sown from May onwards directly into the soil where they are to flower, making a patchwork quilt of colour in every gap.

Useful tricks

Cheat by all means. A large mirror placed at an angle will pick up and reflect plants that are some distance away, giving the impression of additional leaf shapes and colour.

How to design your own skyline

Nature has provided gardeners with an amazing backdrop. The sky, constantly changing and with unforgettable displays in early morning and in the evening close to sunset, is a magnificent canvas to work with, and we should make more of it.

Irrespective of the size of your garden, there is scope to design your own skyline using plants to depict domes, dreaming spires, high-rise office blocks and columns. Late summer is a good time to start thinking about trees and shrubs for ordering in time for autumn planting.

With an eye for detail, your selection of plants can hide unsightly buildings and service poles without detracting from the overall picture. On a balcony, well-positioned container plants can create interest and frame a view. Where a garden slopes up from the house, an intricate line – as though cut with a fretsaw – can be highlighted against the sky. Sun and shade will highlight an ever-changing outline.

Flat gardens with an uninterrupted view to the west are ideal for sunset scenes. Even the bare, wintery tracery of sycamore, chestnut or willow can be effective when the last rays of sunlight slip through gaps in the branches.

When designing your skyline, bear in mind that plants grow at varying rates, with some trees reaching 60ft within 20 years. Colour plays a part with golden conifers, variegated shrubs, autumn leaves and striking bark all combining to create a scene.

Where there is space, trees are an obvious choice, doubling up as a living screen that provides privacy and shelter. It is in your own best interests not to annoy your neighbours. Planting tall, growing trees close to their property or large shrubs that will eventually block their view or reduce daylight will cause grievance.

Deciduous plants

Trees and shrubs that lose their leaves in autumn allow your skyline to evolve over the year. The sturdy, thick branches of an English oak or a network of thin birch twigs can be showstoppers in winter, especially if every limb is outlined with snow. The birch is early into growth, with its green leaves appearing by late March. Oak can be late, often sulking until May. In summer, the steeples of light-green birch and the rounded heads of oak lift the horizon and shape the skyline. By autumn, birch foliage is butter-yellow, contrasting with the orange, red or crimson leaves of rowan, cherry and oak.

Evergreens

Plants that retain their foliage throughout the year are desirable, especially where they are planted to provide shelter and privacy.

An unsightly building will remain hidden rather than making an unwelcome reappearance when leaves are shed. Some evergreens, such as the conifer *Cryptomeria japonica* 'Elegans', will change their leaf colour, the blue-green of summer blushing to red-brown in winter.

Sky high

Where an instant effect is required, take your cheque book to one of the tree and shrub nurseries specialising in large, semi-mature trees. Container-grown trees are readily available up to 16ft high. They may be planted at any time of year, but remember to arrange delivery.

Mature trees that have been prepared for lifting are sold with an enormous root ball secured with hessian and wire mesh. Large specimen trees, shrubs, conifers and bamboos are imported from Northern Italy for sale in garden centres.

Plants with dome-shaped tops include the deciduous weeping birch, *Betula pendula* 'Youngii', which will grow to 25ft with a mushroom-shaped head. *Sorbus intermedia*, the Swedish whitebeam, grows to 35ft, with dark green, deciduous leaves and masses of bright-red berries in autumn.

Pittosporum tenuifolium starts with upright branches but broadens out to form a rounded tree 25ft high with glossy, mid-green, evergreen leaves. It dislikes a cold, windy situation. *Pyrus salicifolia* 'Pendula' is better known as the weeping pear. It has silvery-green, deciduous foliage and grows to 16ft high.

Spire-shaped trees can be dotted throughout the planting where they will stretch above their neighbouring plants.

Another deciduous pear, *Pyrus calleryana* 'Chanticleer', forms a narrow column 20ft high with white flowers in spring. The leaves remain on the tree until early winter. *Prunus* 'Amanogawa' is a delightful, late-spring flowering cherry with fragrant, pale-pink flowers and good yellow, orange and red autumn leaf colour. It remains narrow and upright, reaching 25ft in height.

Tall, thin, columnar conifers include *Juniperus scopulorum* 'Skyrocket' with grey-green foliage, to a height of 20ft. *Juniperus communis* 'Hibernica' is pencil-shaped with mid-green, densely packed, evergreen foliage, reaching 13ft in height.

A large, mature Florence-Court Irish yew, *Taxus baccata* 'Fastigiata', has multiple, stiff, upright stems of dark, evergreen leaves. It will grow to 30ft with a 16ft spread. Its outline against a leaden sky is a reminder of the dreaming spires of Oxford.

When *Fargesia nitida* – fountain bamboo – is allowed to form a clump, it looks magnificent against a cloud-free sky.

A different effect is achieved by planting two columnar, yellow-leafed beech, *Fagus sylvatica* 'Dawyck Gold' 20ft apart. As they grow, train their main stems to a hooped wire so they eventually meet and form a ring. Bearing in mind that this tall, thin variety will reach a height of 60ft, there will be no difficulty achieving a circle. With a little imagination, of course.

How to make a maze

There is no great secret to making your own living garden maze. Just think of it as a collection of hedges. With solid green screens higher than eye level it is easy to lose almost all those who enter.

The design must be committed to paper, with the boundary of the site clearly defined. Use graph paper to make sure you have enough room for both paths and hedges. Remember that plants grow in width as well as height and, taking notice of the growth habit of the species you have chosen, allow for a finished spread of 3ft hedging. Narrow paths can be claustrophobic: a 5ft-wide path will allow you to enjoy the experience.

Planting

Planting a maze is for the long term. You are only doing it once so make sure the roots of the plants are well catered for. Plants are usually close-spaced at 18–24in in the row. It is sometimes more convenient to dig a continuous trench, rather than individual planting holes. Fork up the base to assist drainage and spread a 4in layer of old, rotted farmyard manure. Back-fill with a 2in layer of topsoil and work in a handful of bone-meal fertilizer per yard run of trench.

Use a line to keep the plants straight. Plant at the same depth as previously grown, firming the soil around the roots with your foot.

Providing the ground is not soggy, bare-rooted deciduous shrubs may be planted from late autumn until spring. Container-grown plants may be bought and planted at any time. Water well after planting to settle the soil around the roots.

Aftercare

It is important that the maze retains its foliage to ground level rather than showing its bare legs. The first spring after planting, lightly clip the young plants to encourage side shoots from the base. Regular topping and facing back the sides will thicken and increase the branch system, eventually forming a sturdy, dense screen. Continue to water during the first two seasons and apply a liquid foliar fertilizer in June and August. Mulching will conserve moisture and reduce the need to weed.

Tall-sided mazes involve ladders and extra maintenance. Surfacing the internal paths with bark mulch or compacted gravel provides an all-weather practical surface.

Best plants

Evergreen conifers are hard to beat. They are shapely when trimmed and sufficiently solid to prevent shortcuts or a view through.

Thuja plicata 'Atrovirens', the Western red cedar, makes a quick-growing, dark-green, aromatic screen easily maintained at 6ft high.

Chamaecyparis lawsoniana, Lawson cypress, has a columnar habit. It is quick-growing at 12–14in a year, with bright evergreen foliage. For an instant maze, reasonably priced 4–5ft-high container-grown plants are often available in garden centres.

Taxus baccata, the English yew, has to be the dream maze-maker. Slower-growing, the dark green clipped foliage gives the impression of a solid wall. It is tolerant of abuse but if weeds are allowed to compete, the lower branches will become bare.

Fagus sylvatica, our native beech, is deciduous but retains sufficient russet-brown, dead leaves to form a winter mantle. The new soft-green leaves in spring are worth waiting for.

Carpinus betulus 'Columnaris', the upright hornbeam, is similar to beech with a strong network of branches. In autumn its leaves turn to gold before falling.

Evergreen flowering shrubs such as *Escallonia* 'Donard Radiance' and *Berberis darwinii* are quick growing and make wonderful mazes. Pruning time is critical to allow the plants to produce flowering shoots for the following year. Lightly clip every year after flowering. Even though some varieties of *Escallonia* continue to flower into September, prune in late August and sacrifice some late blossom.

Child's play

Mazes designed for children (see also p. 188) take up less space and will provide plenty of fun. Kept at knee-height, there is a clear view and less opportunity for panic. Summer bedding displays or dwarf shrub beds can be incorporated.

Buxus sempervirens, the common box, with its dark, evergreen leaves is taller growing than the variety 'Suffruticosa'. To date it has shown resistance to the disease which is destroying other varieties all over the country.

Lavender makes a wonderful aromatic maze. A light, well-drained soil is essential. Pruning in spring will encourage lots of summer flower spikes which may be lightly clipped over in autumn.

Santolina cupressocyparis, the cotton lavender, is low-growing with aromatic, soft-grey foliage and masses of bright-yellow, button-like flowerheads in late summer and autumn.

Euonymus fortunei 'Emerald Gold' forms a sturdy, low barrier with evergreen variegated foliage. It tolerates regular clipping. Plain green, reverted branches should be removed.

How to build a maze for children

Turning part of the garden into a safe play area for children, complete with sandpit and play house, is perfectly normal. But what about a maze? Not a grown-up's maze with towering hedges to prevent you seeing over and cheating. For this to work – and mother to be happy – the children must be visible at all times. Low hedges are what's needed.

So select an area, preferably a level one, close to the house and in view of the kitchen or living-room window. Any site that isn't rocky, waterlogged or infested with perennial weeds will be suitable.

A see-through, 3ft perimeter fence of pale fencing will provide additional peace of mind. For safety, fit a gate with its catch out of reach of small hands.

How difficult you make the maze will depend on the ages and capabilities of the children: it should be do-able, but not easy. The whole idea is to keep the children moving about in a small area – a bit like running on the spot. There could be a goal at the finish: a fun piece of equipment such as a Wendy House, or some other incentive.

Design

On graph paper, mark out to scale the lines of hedges and openings. The paths will need to be 4ft wide to accommodate the mature spread of the hedging plants. Doubling back will extend the distance within a small area. Lots of dead ends are part of the fun. When you are happy with the plan, measure the total length of the hedge lines. Divide this by the plant spacing – adding one extra plant for every line – and you have the number of plants required. Order a few extra to allow for plant deaths and accidents.

Best plants

Dense, bushy, low-growing plants that reach a maximum height of 2–3ft are best. A dwarf, evergreen box hedge is an obvious choice. The variety *Buxus sempervirens* 'Suffruticosa' is dwarf, compact and slow growing. Unless the plants are very bushy, space them 10in apart. *Euonymus fortunei* 'Emerald Gaiety' has bright evergreen leaves with white margins. *E. f.* 'Emerald 'n' Gold' is margined in gold. Both varieties will grow to 3ft, but if kept clipped they can be maintained at 2ft. The variegation is attractive in winter. Space the plants 16in apart. *Hypericum kalmianum* is a hardy evergreen shrub with erect stems and blue-green foliage. The saucer-shaped, golden-yellow flowers appear from mid- to late-summer. It grows to a height of 30in but won't withstand rough horseplay. Plant 18in apart.

For something a bit different, plant the maze with *Gaultheria mucronata*. There is a range of varieties, all with small, evergreen leaves and edible winter berries in various colours. Choose from white, pink, cerise and magenta. It will grow to 4ft in height, but can be kept clipped at 3ft. Space the plants 2ft apart. Watch out for suckers, removing any that are growing out into the path.

How to grow

Prepare the planting hole well, adding a balanced, granular fertilizer to encourage quick, healthy growth. Where the plants are close together, dig a continuous trench, into which you should fork well-rotted farmyard manure to retain moisture. Plant firmly and water to settle the soil around the roots. A layer of landscape fabric on the paths will stop weeds growing. This can be surfaced with fine-grade bark mulch, which prevents grazed knees after a fall.

Maintenance

Children have a habit of catching on faster than adults, so if you want to keep them guessing, you will have to cheat. Grow extra hedging plants in grow bags with added sterilized soil. Each bag will give a 3ft length of identical hedge. Use these to fill gaps the children have become accustomed to, and remove other sections to make new gaps. Watering is essential to prevent the plants drying out. Eventually the children will tire of the sport. While you wait for the grandchildren, turn the area into a vegetable and herb potager with ready-made boundary hedges.

PART IV
Cushnie Comment

New Year resolutions 2010

This year I fully intend planting just three tomato plants and a single cucumber. Last year I could have cornered the local market. The tomatoes were in hanging baskets, pots, double growing bags and in the greenhouse soil. A single cucumber plant had 18 fruit and cucumber sandwiches are not my scene. It has to be said that all the tomatoes tasted good but it was those in hanging baskets that were blight-free. Perhaps the spores are like carrot fly – afraid of heights.

I am determined to encourage more gardeners to grow posh vegetables. Now that home-grown has caught on it is time to move away from boring cabbage and other rabbit food. Enjoy the finer things in life. Grow globe and Jerusalem artichoke, sweet corn and asparagus.

I have decided to count the number of lettuce seeds I sow. Last year there was a lot of waste. We can use about 8–10 before they bolt. If I sow 20 seeds that allows for poor germination, feeding snails and giving a few to friends. With between 500 and 1,500 seeds in a packet there is a fair chance that I will never need to buy another one.

Until last year I was opposed to planting an olive tree. Lovely leaf, nice flower but no need to buy a press. Then I was asked to try new cultivars that are supposed to be hardy in Britain. I now have two olive trees 'Veronique' and 'Peace'. One of them has produced a few black olives so I am going to plant some more. If I have my way the island of Ireland will soon be buoyant on virgin olive oil or sinking under a weight of useless trees.

We all know how to avoid it but I am forever planting on top of hibernating bulbs. I see a gap that is just right for my new purchase. In goes the spade and up come beheaded autumn flowering bulbs. From now on I will mark each bulb site with a layer of fine gravel. However, there is always the risk of thinking it is the ideal position for something needing a free-draining soil.

Another 'must not do' is to convince myself that there will be sufficient room to plant rampant climbers in a constricted space. Some of my favourites are barely controllable. *Vitis coignetiae*, *Clematis montana* f. *grandiflora* and *Rosa* 'Wedding Day' will, given time, make a bungalow disappear. With me, *Clematis armandii* jumps from tree to tree giving deciduous trees an evergreen canopy and drizzling down its wonderful scent on the unwary but, in truth, it should never have been there in the first place.

Regarding the pond I am definitely going to dunk the barley straw early in spring. It really needs to be submerged for six weeks before becoming effective. It doesn't half look funny pushed into a pair of old tights with a brick to weigh it down and the lower 'legs' hanging out of the water.

Last year was an awful season for blight so this year I am planting the Sarpo potato varieties 'Mira' and 'Axona'. Ireland can't afford another famine.

It's neither laziness nor stupidity but usually I am soaked when giving the grass its last cut of the year. You know, the cut that will leave the lawn looking good for the rest of the winter but the rain comes on before you finish. You can't wait to get dry and forget to clean out the grass box. Weeks or months later it has dried and hardened to a crust that seems glued to every metal part. From now on if it looks like rain we both stay inside.

I'm working on a plan to help me remember where I put last year's left-over seed. There are so many sensible places and the packets are never where I thought they should be. The strange thing is I will find them when storing this year's half-empty packets. When I'm at it I want a see-through cupboard so that I don't miss the gladioli that I lifted, dried and stored. When the green shoots of recovery are pushing out of brown paper bags and reused orange nets it is really too late.

I want to encourage you all, when you are buying plants, to check their labels for spread as well as height. More plants are lost through overcrowding than by their height.

If I can remember to I am resolved to net some berries of holly, *Gaultheria* and *Pyracantha* next November to stop the darling little feathered friends devouring the lot before the festive season. From now on, and I said it last year as well, I am going to remove seed heads of mullein, foxglove and lady's mantle before they scatter themselves all over the garden doubling the weeding problem.

I have a walnut tree that is 30 years old. It has never produced a single nut but already has timber value. I am going to plant one of the new varieties such as *Juglans regia* 'Rita' that produce fruit within four to five years. The existing tree I will leave in my will.

I am very bad at labelling seeds and cuttings. I know what they are. The trouble is if there is no germination or all the cuttings die (it won't be my fault) there is no clue. When I master the technique of always using a label I will know what not to bother with next year.

One final New Year's resolution. I am not going to question what I am told. The weather will be as prophesied, the new roses will be resistant to black spot, the tomatoes will have a fantastic flavour and the sweet corn will ripen early. In truth one of the things that make a good gardener is the ability to ignore a lot of nonsense. I hope this wasn't a waste of your time!

New Year resolutions 2007

Naturally I know the names of the plants in my garden, but I keep finding weeds that are unfamiliar; so in 2007 I am going to identify and label them. By the time I've finished, my garden will contain more labelled plants than most botanic gardens.

On changes to BBC Gardeners' World

I was knee-high to a pretty big grasshopper when I watched Percy Thrower demonstrate the proper way to use hedge clippers – where to stand, how to hold them, how to cut straight and the resultant immaculate conifer screen. It was all basic gardening information on how to carry out a simple task. But a task only becomes simple when you know how to do it properly. I am still good with hand-held clippers and enjoy using them.

Then there was Geoffrey Smith. A serious case of been-there-done-that. Remember when he physically planted an annual border down at Clack's Farm? It has never been better done. Still at the farm, Arthur Billett consistently grew the best tomatoes I have ever seen and showed millions how to do it his way. Geoff Hamilton's cheap and practical garden frame became the in thing for every gardener. Bob Flowerdew wrestling with a car tyre served a useful purpose: garage owners still thank him for reducing their piles of rubber. Generations have grown and grown up with *Gardeners' World*. It has, over the decades, been the flagship of practical gardening.

Makeovers, trendy gimmicks, bright colours, mass concrete, glass, mirrors and acres of timber are all very well, but keen gardeners garden because plants and soil go together. Novices want to be stimulated by do-able projects and practical jobs that are easily implemented in their own gardens. As it happens, this also makes for watchable television.

Now there is to be a change in the nation's favourite television programme on gardening. There will be new people at the BBC deciding which items will be featured, how they will be covered and what kind of gardener they are aimed at.

Is it too much to ask that the hands-on approach and practical demonstrations are not only retained but, where the presenters are capable, they are extended at the expense of ephemera? Surely it isn't necessary to point out to anyone that 99 per cent of gardens are tended by amateurs, many of whom are keen to the point that they watch *Gardeners' World* with the aim of learning something and, with luck, doing better.

There is also a change in presenter. I sincerely wish Montagu Don the very best. I am absolutely certain he will want to carry on the incredibly high standards of professionalism set by his predecessors.

Remember how the press and, I'm sure, some of the public tried to prune Alan Titchmarsh. With his trademark common sense and dignity he rose above it and became, quite rightly, the nation's gardener. Alan brought changes but he had the skill and was allowed the time to explain and demonstrate, in simple terms and actions, the fundamentals of gardening.

When Pippa Greenwood shows you how to sow seeds or plant vegetables you not only learn how to do it but you also want to go straight out and try it for yourself. That sort of expertise can only be dispensed by an expert.

Mr Don will no doubt make changes and that will be good. He will be different from those who have gone before and we will get used to that. It is rumoured that he is a fancy dresser – it would be a shame, however, if he didn't need boots, a waterproof coat and the occasional sticking plaster.

Titchmarsh is now doing his own thing, making the most of his ability to get his message across while giving viewers the confidence to go out and garden. With the help of clever camera work, his suggestions and ideas are easy to follow and to put into practice, just as they were on *Gardeners' World*.

With its new captain, there is no reason why the *Gardeners' World* flagship shouldn't continue to rule the air waves, however. If the writers, presenters, their producers and the channel controllers remember that actions speak louder than words, we are sure to remain a nation of gardeners.

What I want to see at Chelsea Flower Show 2005

What will my first stop be? I don't so much make a bee-line as flutter about like a butterfly. I hate missing anything but a must this year is the Cayeux stand, which is a famous French nursery specialising in irises. If you want to grow them then these are the people to visit. With garden relaxation in mind, I also want to check out any new hard surfaces.

And what would I like to see more of? Space – but that, I suppose, comes under the heading 'prayer'. More small-garden designs would be good, especially if they were plant-orientated and designed with low maintenance in mind. I could do without new plant varieties that are claimed to be 'the best-ever'. After growing them for a season we come to realize that they are neither disease-resistant, hardy, nor vigorous and certainly not fit to be exhibited at Chelsea Flower Show.